THE WORLD OF THE
SEA OTTER

THE WORLD OF THE
SEA OTTER

Text by Stefani Paine

Photographs by Jeff Foott

Sierra Club Books
San Francisco

The Sierra Club, founded in 1892 by John Muir, has devoted itself to the study and protection of the Earth's scenic and ecological resources — mountains, wetlands, woodlands, wild shores and rivers, deserts and plains. The publishing program of the Sierra Club offers books to the public as a nonprofit educational service in the hope that they may enlarge the public's understanding of the Club's basic concerns. The point of view expressed in each book, however, does not necessarily represent that of the Club. The Sierra Club has some sixty chapters coast to coast, in Canada, Hawaii, and Alaska. For information about how you may participate in its programs to preserve wilderness and the quality of life, please address inquiries to Sierra Club, 730 Polk Street, San Francisco, CA 94109.

Sierra Club Books paperback edition: 1995

Published in Canada by Greystone Books, a division of Douglas & McIntyre Ltd., 1615 Venables Street, Vancouver, British Columbia V5L 2H1

Library of Congress Cataloging-in-Publication Data
Paine, Stefani, 1946–
    Sea Otters / Stefani Paine
        p.   cm.
    Includes bibliographical references and index,
    ISBN 0-87156-375-4
    1. Sea Otter.   I. Title
  QL737.C25P24 1993
   599.74'447—dc20   93-2820
                            CIP

The quotation on page 107 is from *Hunters of the Stormy Sea* by Harold McCracken (Garden City, N.Y: Doubleday, 1957). Reprinted by permission of the publisher.

Edited by Nancy Flight
Design by Barbara Hodgson
Maps by Lisa Ireton
Printed and bound in Hong Kong by C & C Offset Printing Co., Ltd.
10 9 8 7 6 5 4 3 2 1

FOR MICHAEL

CONTENTS

ACKNOWLEDGEMENTS

I am indebted to the great number of scientists and biologists who over the years have laboured in the field and in laboratories in search of the scientific truth as it relates to sea otters. With each new discovery or observation, another piece is added to the puzzle and a clearer picture of the sea otter and its biology emerges. I am indebted as well to some writers of history, now dead, who wrote their accounts of events at the time of the great fur hunt with boldness, honesty and emotion.

My sincere thanks go to the many people who helped in large and small ways with this book: Lee Wright, Brad Andrews, Andy Lamb, Margaret Butschler, Gil Hewlett, Candace Savage, Dave Powell, Robin Fisher and Colin Savage. A particular debt is owed to Rob Sanders for initiating the project and to Nancy Flight for her guidance and editing skills.

INTRODUCTION

My first encounter with a wild sea otter occurred two decades ago. It was a cool, bright afternoon in December at a marina near Monterey, California. I was the guest of some colleagues from that area, and we were loading a large motorboat with plastic bins filled with supplies. As I was stowing clothing, food and camera gear, a movement in the water just in front of the boat caught my eye. There it was—a real, live sea otter.

I knew the animal's remarkable history and some of its biology. I knew that this smallest of marine mammals had been hunted to near-extinction hundreds of years ago, that a few pockets of sea otters had survived in the Aleutian Islands and that a small colony had been found off the coast of California near Big Sur. I knew that the sea otter's fur was denser by far than that of any other animal and that this remarkable fur was the sea otter's protection against the chilly coastal waters. I also knew that the sea otter was rare, and I never expected to see one in the wild. To see this animal was like seeing a living legend.

The animal cruised by the boat on its back in typical sea otter fashion. A deliberate sweep of its broad hind flipper now and then propelled the otter with ease between the boats, dock pilings and loosely tethered dinghies. It swam, then rolled forward, dived, reappeared and continued to patrol the area. Unlike most wild animals, this sea otter was neither nervous nor anxious. Its eyes registered my presence as a fact, not a threat.

I put my bin down and gave my full attention to watching the sea otter. When it lifted its head and turned its face in my direction, I saw a dark brown, broad, furry face, an oversized bushy mustache, a big black nose and intelligent dark eyes. There was no suspicion, hostility or aggression in its expression, just a relaxed confidence. It was an engaging, attractive face, and it quietly drew me in to the sea otter's world.

Although sea otters congregate in rafts at resting sites, all other activities, such as hunting, mating and giving birth, take place apart from the group.

1

Although I later met other sea otters, no meeting matched the power of that first encounter, until one day in the early summer of 1989. On that very special day, I held a baby sea otter in my arms. Its plump little body pressed itself against my chest and squirmed comfortably in my cradled arms. Its tiny furry face nuzzled into my neck, and its soft, silky little paws quickly investigated my nose and ears and the collar of my shirt. The otter touched and nuzzled my buttons, hair, pockets and earrings, all the while emitting happy coos, grunts and baby squeaks. A pure, tender joy bubbled up inside me, and I laughed and loved that little sea otter with the depth of my being.

Annie, as she was named, was three months old. She was an orphan, and she should never have been where she was. She belonged in the cool, wild ocean with her wise and caring mother, learning all about what it was to be a sea otter. She should have been learning to dive, to hunt for food on the sea bottom and to dig for clams. She should have been learning how to find protected resting places on an ever-moving sea, and where and when to migrate to find food in season. But Annie had no mother. She had been killed in the infamous *Exxon Valdez* oil spill in March 1989. As a consequence, Annie would spend her entire life being cared for by human caretakers. Without the skills she could learn only at her mother's side during those first vital months, Annie could never survive in the sea. Annie was alive, but she would never be free.

Annie and another pup had been rescued in Alaska, flown to the Monterey Bay Aquarium and cared for there with great competence and devotion. When the pups outgrew the nursery facilities in Monterey, they were flown by private jet to the Vancouver Aquarium, and that is where I met Annie. Had she been orphaned ten or twenty years earlier, she would never have survived—not because nobody cared, but because nobody knew how to care for her. Most of what we know about sea otter behaviour, biology and physiology has come to light in the past two decades. Thus, although Annie is living proof of humankind's power to destroy, her survival is a testimony to science, as well as to the care and devotion that some people are willing to give to protect wild living things.

This book tells the story of the sea otter. It is the story of how this animal with the beautiful fur, engaging manner and distinctive lifestyle makes its living in chilly coastal seas. At every moment and in every way, the ocean is as vital as air to the sea otter's survival. This book also tells the story of the sea otter at the hand of human beings, from the hunters who drove the otters to near-extinction to those who worked to return the sea otter to its vast ancestral range.

The story of the sea otter is a success story. Now sea otters are legally protected and are thriving in areas where they have been absent for a very long time. The sea otters are doing their part; it remains to be seen whether we, as both the greatest protectors and the greatest destroyers of wildlife, will continue to do our part to ensure the peace and prosperity of this magnificent creature.

PART I

At Home in the Sea

CHAPTER 1

A Unique Lifestyle

No one knows how the sea otter evolved. One can speculate that the ancestral sea otter was an entrepreneur looking around for a better way to make a living. The sea otter's ancestor was a terrestrial mammal grubbing around here and there, endlessly looking for food and shelter, protection from enemies, a mate and a safe place to rear young. One can assume that many other mammalian species were looking for exactly the same things, resulting in a lot of competition for land-based resources.

Instead of foraging for plants or small, edible animals on land, otters along the coast began to forage at the seashore. Low tide laid out an array of mussels, snails, urchins and limpets. Food was abundant and easily gathered. This was good, and it got better when the otter discovered there was even more to eat underwater. Gradually the ancestral otter waded deeper and deeper into the sea. Soon it began to swim and dive for snails, crabs and even slow-moving fish. By swimming and diving, the otter could eat whenever it wanted, not just at low tide. Swimming meant it could cover more territory faster. But best of all, no other mammal had exploited the new niche. It was virgin territory.

The ancestral sea otter had found a terrific source of food, and it could swim and dive and rest on the surface. But it could not keep warm enough in cold water, which draws off body heat ten times faster than air.

Many mammals that live in a cool climate have fur coats that shed rain and wrap the animal in a permanent and efficient insulating blanket during the months of cold. These fur coats provide warmth not by their weight but by trapping air in their fine underfur. The trapped air is the insulator. (The principle is identical to that of a down jacket.) When warm weather arrives, the animal sheds much of the underfur, changing its winter coat into a lighter, more comfortable summer dress.

This system works beautifully in air, but it is useless in water. A woollen sweater

PAGES 8–9: One good shake leaves the otter's fur remarkably dry.

FACING PAGE: Good sea otter habitat has rocky coastal shores with reefs and islets for shelter and abundant marine organisms for food.

under a raincoat will keep you warm and dry when you go sailing on a cool day. But if you fall into the water, the heavy clothing provides no warmth and its wet weight becomes a real liability. The difficulty of keeping warm in cold water is probably why so few mammals returned to exploit the sea's riches; they couldn't keep warm while they were fishing. The more highly evolved whales, dolphins, seals and sea lions solved the problem by wrapping their bodies in a layer of blubber. But what about the sea otter?

The ancestral sea otter had probably already lived in northern latitudes and had a handsome fur coat with dense underfur and longer guard hairs over its head and back. The guard hairs would provide a rain cape in the winter wet. Over time, the underfur became finer and denser, trapping more air in its fibres until it became a downy blanket. The guard hairs grew long enough to cover the soft underfur in a smooth, even coat and dense enough to form a waterproof coating that prevented water from penetrating the dry underfur. In this way, the sea otter evolved a coat that would keep its body buoyant, warm and dry. Now it could spend all its time in the sea, eating, visiting, playing, mating and rearing its young—all because of its waterproof coat.

The sea otter's coat is without equal among furred animals. With up to 164,000 fibres per square centimetre (1,062,000 per square inch), the sea otter's coat is twice as dense as that of the next most densely furred mammal, the fur seal. (An entire head of human hair averages 100,000 hairs.) Sea otter fur is so dense that it doesn't drape. Imagine the most luxurious, shimmering velvet that is as cool as silk and as soft as powder.

The individual hairs of the sea otter's fur can only form a waterproof barrier if they are absolutely clean. If hairs are soiled and stick together in clumps, the waterproofing is lost, the barrier leaks and the underfur is wetted. Then the animal becomes chilled and dies. There is little wonder that sea otters are fastidious in their grooming. Every centimetre of the sea otter's coat must be attended to. The coat is scrubbed, licked clean and combed. The air layer is renewed by drying and blowing. Like a toddler's blanket sleeper, the sea otter's coat is large and loose so that every part of it can be pulled around the otter's mouth and paws to be groomed.

In addition to its marvellous waterproof coat, the sea otter developed other adaptations to life in the sea. It developed long webbed toes on its hind feet, creating large swimming flippers. Like all other marine mammals, the sea otter has a high metabolic rate. The sea otter also has a lung capacity that is $2\frac{1}{2}$ times that of an equivalent-sized land mammal; bigger lungs mean greater buoyancy when resting at the surface and better oxygen capacity for diving. Finally, the sea otter does not need to drink fresh water.

THE BIOLOGY OF THE SEA OTTER

NEXT PAGE: *Wrapped in a wonderfully dense fur coat, the sea otter is protected from the ocean's chill.*

PAGES 16–17: *Washing up after dinner.*

Sea otters are mammals, meaning that they give birth to live young who are nourished on milk from female mammary glands. Within the class Mammalia, sea otters belong to the order Carnivora, along with dogs, cats, bears and hyenas, to name a few other members. Within this order, sea otters belong to the family Mustelidae, along with weasels, mink, skunks and about eleven other species of otters.

The sea otter, *Enhydra lutris*, is the only member of the family Mustelidae that is a true marine mammal, or a mammal that lives exclusively in the sea. Aquatic mammals, such as river otters and beavers, use water for food or protection but move around on land, bear their young on land and must drink fresh water.

River otters are common in protected coastal areas, drawn there by the abundance of food in the rocky tidal and subtidal areas. Because river otters may feed, play and swim on the seashore, they are often incorrectly assumed to be sea otters. Their presence on the seashore does not make them sea otters, however, and the two species are quite different both in physical appearance and in behaviour. A river otter, *Lutra canadensis*, at 120 centimetres (47 inches), is a little shorter than the sea otter, but it is much slimmer. The river otter weighs only 6 to 10 kilograms (13 to 22 pounds), whereas the sea otter weighs 20 to 40 kilograms (44 to 88 pounds). The river otter's fur is shorter and smoother, and its tail is thick and round at the base, tapering quickly to a conical point. On shore, river otters are agile, weasel-like in profile, quick, boisterous and playful. Whole families, consisting of an adult pair and their two, three or four kits, are often seen together. River otters always den on land at night. As seafood eaters with casual toilet habits, river otters occupy dens that are smelled long before they are seen.

In contrast, the sea otter is seldom—and in some areas never—seen on shore. When it is out of water, it is awkward, lumbering and clumsy; its big hind flippers step on each other and get in the way. A sea otter family consists of a mother and her single pup, and they do not den on land at night but sleep on their backs in the water. The sea otter has essentially severed all ties with its terrestrial past. It can live its entire life in the sea, eating, sleeping, giving birth and rearing its young without ever coming on shore.

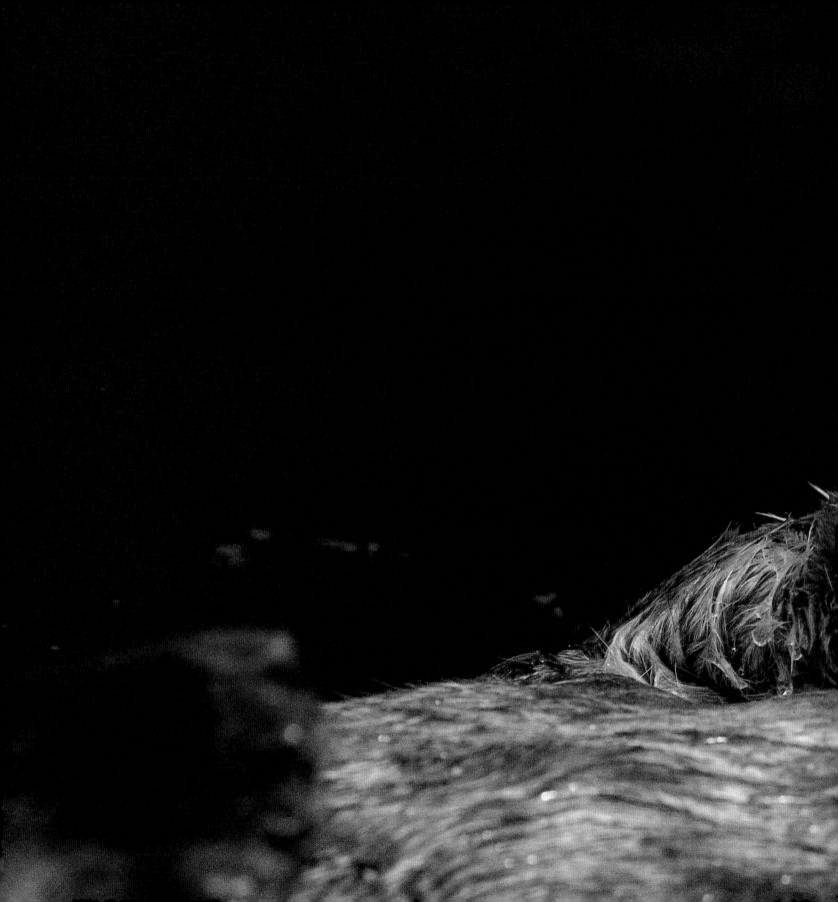

A sea otter grooms its marvellous coat from top to bottom.

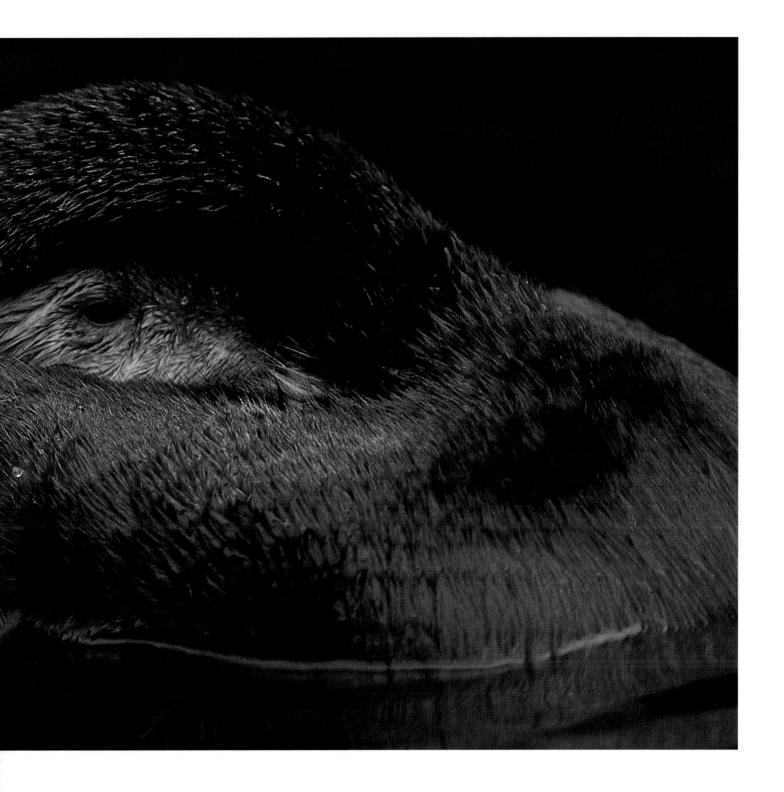

Fossil records from the early and late Pleistocene suggest that modern sea otters evolved in the northeast Pacific in association with cool-water faunas in areas of shallow to moderate depth near islands. Fossil remains have been found in Oregon, central and southern California, and Baja Caifornia, Mexico.

The sea otter's "original range" typically refers to where otters were found and later hunted to near-extinction after they were discovered by Europeans in 1741. This range extended from the Japanese Archipelago north to the Kuril Islands, the Kamchatka Peninsula and the Commander Islands. Sea otters were also found on the islands of the Aleutian chain east to the Alaska Peninsula and then south along the coast of North America to Baja California in Mexico.

Before they were discovered by Europeans, sea otters were certainly known to many different people living along the coast. The Aleuts of the Aleutian chain, for example, have lived on these islands for more than eight thousand years. They used to wear a long, shirt-like garment made of sea otter fur or bird feathers, which the Europeans named the parka. Sea otter fur was also used by other native groups living on the Pacific coast.

Before the great commercial hunt, there were an estimated 150,000 to 300,000 sea otters scattered throughout the historical range. By 1911, when sea otters came under the protection of the Fur Seal Agreement, 170 years after the beginning of the commercial hunt, the total population of sea otters had declined to a mere 1,000 to 2,000 animals in thirteen remnant populations.

Today sea otters have recovered and occupy most of their historical range from the Kuril Islands northeast to Prince William Sound, Alaska. On the Pacific coast, transplanted populations thrive in southeastern Alaska and in some spots in British Columbia and Washington. Central California also has populations of sea otters. It is estimated that there are 150,000 or more sea otters alive today; however, they are doing better in some areas than in others. For example, from a handful of sea otters in the Kuril Islands, 6,000 to 7,000 are living there now. In contrast, California is estimated to have had 16,000 to 20,000 sea otters historically, yet today only 1,800 to 2,000 can be found.

How is it that the diminutive sea otter could range so successfully over such a huge expanse of ocean and between such disparate climates as those of Mexico and Alaska? Above water there is a dramatic difference between the mild temperatures and waving palm trees of Mexico or Southern California and the bleak, windswept islands of the

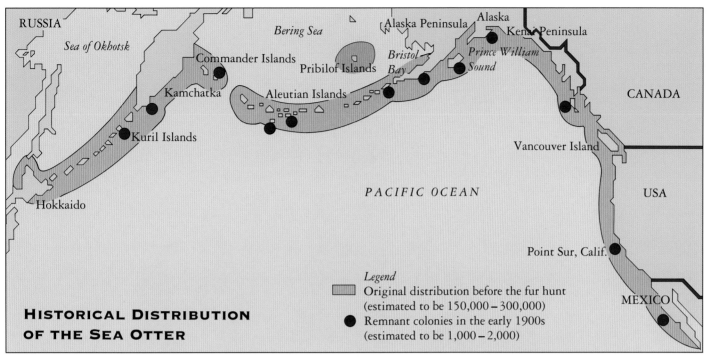

RUSSIA

Sea of Okhotsk

Bering Sea

Commander Islands

Pribilof Islands

Alaska Peninsula

Alaska

Kenai Peninsula

Bristol Bay

Prince William Sound

Kamchatka

Aleutian Islands

CANADA

Kuril Islands

Vancouver Island

Hokkaido

PACIFIC OCEAN

USA

Point Sur, Calif.

Legend
Original distribution before the fur hunt
(estimated to be 150,000 – 300,000)
● Remnant colonies in the early 1900s
(estimated to be 1,000 – 2,000)

MEXICO

**HISTORICAL DISTRIBUTION
OF THE SEA OTTER**

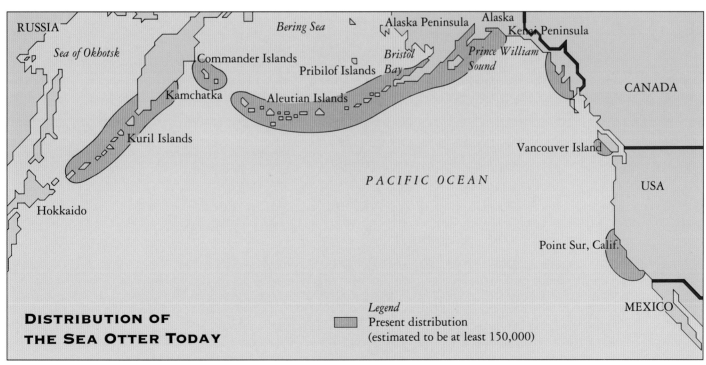

RUSSIA

Bering Sea

Alaska Peninsula

Alaska

Sea of Okhotsk

Commander Islands

Pribilof Islands

Bristol Bay

Kenai Peninsula

Prince William Sound

Kamchatka

Aleutian Islands

CANADA

Kuril Islands

Vancouver Island

Hokkaido

PACIFIC OCEAN

USA

Point Sur, Calif.

MEXICO

**DISTRIBUTION OF
THE SEA OTTER TODAY**

Legend
Present distribution
(estimated to be at least 150,000)

Aleutians. Underwater, however, there is a surprising uniformity of temperature. This is because waters in the North Pacific are warmed by the Kuroshio Current as it flows northward along the coast of North America. As a result, an abundance of marine invertebrate organisms, which make up the sea otter's diet, occurs throughout the range. In addition, although air temperatures along the Aleutian chain may plummet in deep winter, the water will not freeze. Sea otters cannot survive north of here in areas that ice over in the winter because they must have access to open water to forage.

FACING PAGE: Sea otters share their coastal habitat with playful sea lions.

NEXT PAGE: The sea in all its fury or all its calm is the sea otter's home.

CHOOSING A HOME

Although sea otters are true marine mammals, you will not find them living far out to sea. Instead you will find them in coastal areas where water depth is less than 30 metres (100 feet). The reason for this is that sea otters collect their food from the sea bottom. They are strong swimmers and good divers, but every trip to the sea floor and back is a long round trip on a single breath of air. Under great stress, a sea otter can hold its breath for up to five minutes. On average, though, sea otters stay submerged for thirty to ninety seconds.

The shallower the water, the less time spent travelling and the more time spent collecting food. The deeper the water, the more time spent travelling and the less time available for hunting. At some point, it is no longer practical for the sea otter to dive deeper, even though it is capable of doing so. Sea otters can dive to at least 45 metres (150 feet), but they seem to favour water depths of half that.

The sea otter also requires protection from changing tides, currents and winds. When, as casual visitors to the seashore, we stand on the beach and look out to the ocean, we see a vast, faceless deep. We are typically there on a pleasant day, since that is when we are most likely to want to go for a walk on the beach. The sea otter experiences the sea on the same soft day as we do. Unlike us, though, the otter is still there in the evening when the tide shifts, and on into the night when the winds begin to rise. As the breeze gathers speed, falters and returns with great breathy gusts, it transforms the calm surface water into a twisted fury. There are no people on the beach. Even small birds and other animals have taken shelter from the wind. But what of the little sea otter rising and falling on the untidy waves, a sloppy crest dousing its nose and face with cold salt water?

The sea otter lives straddled between two worlds. It lives with us in the world of sun-

shine and air. As it lounges on its back in the low swells, it can see us on shore. Like us, it feels the warmth of the sun on its face and takes in deep, clean breaths of air. But the sea otter also lives in an underwater world where we cannot easily go. There it hunts in the silent underwater kelp jungle. It swims easily among the bizarre life forms of the kelp forest, the low, lush algae pastures and the sandy plains pocked with the breathing holes of clams, shrimp and worms. The sea otter lives in the interface of these two worlds, the world of water and the world of air.

The sea otter lives on and in the sea all day, every day, with wind, current and tide. Yet like its terrestrial cousins tucked snug and dry under an old cedar stump, the sea otter needs a sheltered place to rest. It needs easily accessible places where it can groom or sleep without being blown about or carried out to sea. It finds such refuges on a broken shore where scattered offshore rocks and reefs dampen the waves and where bays and inlets afford protection from current and tides.

The sea otter's home, then, is not simply the sea; it is a special part of the sea. It is a coastal area of a certain depth, which is determined by the otter's diving range. It also has the kinds of plants and animals living on its sea bottom that will offer up abundant food for the otter. Finally, it contains islands, inlets, rocks and reefs to act as natural breakwaters. Here and there over thousands of convoluted coastal kilometres from northern Mexico to Alaska and across the North Pacific, sea otters have found this combination of conditions. We call this sea otter habitat. They would call it home.

Kelp beds are good resting areas. Strong yet elastic kelp plants are used as anchor lines, preventing a resting otter from drifting with wind and tide.

27

CHAPTER 2

Behold the Banquet

Imagine waking up one morning and finding yourself sitting on a remote beach somewhere—let us say in the Queen Charlotte Islands. The day is bright and fresh. New spring grass moves in the sea breeze, and bird sounds come in spurts from the woods behind you. You gaze about, rise, stretch a bit and begin walking. Soon a growing hunger creeps into your consciousness, and you begin to think of food. In this fantasy, you have been set down at your beach location without provisions: no sandwiches, no thermos of coffee, no sweet rolls. Neither have you been provided with even the most elementary equipment that might help you harvest something to eat. You have no fish hooks, no nets, no rods, no knife, no axe. You have no matches, paper or wood. And you have no restaurant, supermarket or kitchen. Imagine that you have only yourself—your hands, your feet and your wits—and you must somehow make a living for yourself, finding enough food each day to sustain yourself and provide energy for other important day-to-day activities: avoiding danger and possible predators, and finding a mate. Think of how much you eat in the course of one day and try to imagine collecting that each and every day off the beach. If you are female, you will need even more nourishment. Consider, too, that if you don't feel well one morning, you go foraging anyway, or you don't eat.

This is the daily challenge of all animals in the wild, including the sea otter. This animal must work even harder at finding food than you would, since it eats 20 to 25 per cent of its body weight each day.

Using its forepaws along with its teeth and strong jaws, the sea otter can break apart food items that are too large to be eaten whole.

A sea otter swims to the surface through a kelp forest holding a large sea urchin and a rock to break it open.

Somewhere in the distance, you hear a series of sharp, rapid clicks. Moving in on the scene, you spot a sea otter floating on its back, a clam held firmly between two flat paws, and a blur of short arms working together as the sea otter bangs the clam on its chest, as if driving a spike with both arms. Coming closer, you see a good-sized rock cradled in the animal's chest fur. The sea otter uses it like an anvil, repeatedly banging the clam on it. At last the banging stops, and after a rapid roll in the water, the otter is eating the clam. Quickly, mouth, teeth and paws are working together. The otter tosses pieces of shell aside as its strong, white teeth scrape off the fleshy bits. There is more chewing, followed by another quick roll, and the sea otter reappears with another clam, like a magician pulling a coin from the air. The entire process is repeated until four or five good-size clams have been cracked open and consumed. Another roll and the rock disappears. Now the sea otter will groom and rest.

Returning three or four hours later when the sea otter is ready to eat again, you might find it collecting heavy-shelled snails, spidery crabs, thousand-spined sea urchins, Chinese hat limpets, deep blue mussels, a black leathery chiton, a rock scallop, a flatfish or a ragged tube worm. You might see it chew the arm off an orange sea star or pull a reluctant hermit crab from its shell.

The sea otter is an efficient hunter and will collect and eat just about any fish or invertebrate animal it can find. Other true marine mammals, including whales, dolphins, seals and sea lions, have the advantage of speed and range. They can chase and catch fast-moving fish, which they swallow underwater. Although the sea otter is too slow for most fish, except the sluggish bottom fish species, it has a great advantage in being able to use its forepaws. In contrast, seals and dolphins can eat only what they can catch with their jaws alone. And unless they bite off a chunk of something, they are limited to what they can swallow whole. These animals also catch and swallow underwater, "on the fly." The sea otter always eats at the surface, spreading its bounty on its chest, as if it were a lunch counter.

The sea otter plays and rests on the sea's surface, but it hunts on the sea floor. In readiness for a dive, the otter sucks in a full breath of air and rolls forward in one strong and graceful turn. Now an invisible clock begins to tick. Seconds march by as the otter holds its forepaws across its chest and propels itself downward with powerful undulations of its body, hind flippers held together and spread in a dolphin-like pose. The clock continues to tick. Now on the sea bottom, the otter navigates with great flexibility by alternate sweeps of its hind flippers and overhand pulls with its forearms. As the otter spots urchins, crabs or other edibles, it swiftly tucks them into loose skin folds under each arm, which act like built-in shopping bags. Tick, tick—time is almost out as the otter runs out of air. The otter has worked hard, swimming down perhaps 18 or 20 metres (60 or 66 feet), moved quickly, searched for and collected food, making the most of precious seconds before it is forced to the surface to breathe. If the trip had not been successful, the otter would dive again and again in successive trips of thirty, sixty or ninety seconds.

On another trip, it might use its sensitive whiskers to locate small crabs or snails hidden in the dense seaweed mats, or reach into crevices and pat under boulders with equally sensitive forepaws, feeling for low-profile limpets or chitons hidden from view. The sea otter's paws are a little like flat mitts. They do not look particularly agile or manipulative, but they are. Combined with short, semi-retractable claws, the paws are surprisingly strong and agile. Otters will use both paws together to rub, roll, twist and pull with great strength and dexterity. Playing with the young sea otters that had been hand-reared after their mothers had died in the *Exxon Valdez* oil spill, I learned just how mobile and efficient these paws could be. The otters loved to nuzzle and feel everything. They could remove rings from fingers in an instant and steal buttons, belts and objects in pockets with the slick ease of a pickpocket. A tug of war over a set of keys demonstrated the sea otter's surprising strength for its size.

This great dexterity is of enormous advantage when searching out and collecting smaller food items. Sea otters can comb kelp fronds in search of kelp crabs and snails or, underwater, search in the complicated kelp's holdfast for the many creatures that seek refuge there.

The sea otter's skill at collecting abalone has not only angered commercial abalone divers but also challenged biologists trying to determine how this small animal can dislodge the huge, flat snails. Abalone have two avenues of defence: a large, heavy shell and the power to clamp down with great force when disturbed. It is estimated that an abalone may exert a suction equal to four thousand times its own weight. Abalone divers use a flat iron bar as a crowbar to dislodge the abalone, which can be as much as 15 to 25 centimetres (6 to 10 inches) across and contain up to a kilogram (a couple of pounds) of body meat. Underwater observations reveal that the sea otter uses a stone about the size of a large softball to dislodge the abalone. Holding the stone in both paws, the sea otter uses it to hammer the side of the abalone shell at the rate of forty-five blows in fifteen seconds. Abalone are big, thick shelled and tough. Sea otters are persistent, determined and wilful. Although it may take one, two or even three episodes of abalone bashing, eventually the sea otter emerges with its prize.

Sea otters are also great clam diggers, successfully collecting a variety of species, from the prized pismo clam to smaller sand clams and razor clams. Clams do not sit on the sand waiting to be picked up by the sea otter any more than they sit on the sand waiting to be picked up by recreational diggers. Clams must be dug. Since the clams live embedded in the sand 10 to 50 centimetres (4 to 20 inches) below the surface, the sea otter begins by digging a trench. Working head down and using its forepaws to dig, much like a dog digs in the sand, the sea otter excavates a trench in a series of short, energetic digging sessions of about half a minute each. Subsequent dives enlarge the trench, as the sea otter digs into the side of the trench searching for clams. In the end, the trench may be 0.5 metre (1½ feet) deep and wide and 1.5 metres (5 feet) long. Since the largest clams are generally the deepest, this deep digging makes sense. For example, the butter clam, *Saxidomus giganteus*, lives as deep as 50 centimetres (20 inches).

The sea otter's eagerness to explore anything and everything within its environment as a source of food is somewhat unusual in an adult animal. This characteristic has no doubt contributed to its ability to thrive over such an extensive geographical range. The food species eaten in the Aleutians, for example, are not the same as those eaten in California. This constant search and determination to exploit potential food sources is well illustrated by an otter observed in Monterey Bay that had made the connection between discarded soft drink cans and small octopuses. Young octopuses will seek shelter in any crevice offering a small entrance and protection from predators. Since octopuses are soft bodied except for their hard, parrot-like beak, they can squeeze themselves through the smallest openings, the size of which is determined by the size of their beaks. In the same way that a large, flaccid, water-filled balloon could be worked through a very small hole, an octopus can gain entry through very small openings. It is not surprising that small octopuses in Monterey Bay have taken up residence in discarded cans.

Biologists watching sea otters in Monterey Bay in the 1970s saw a sea otter bite open a pop can. Within the next fifteen minutes, seven more cans were retrieved, five of which contained octopuses. It took the otter an average of thirty seconds to open each can. Divers checking the area later discovered twenty-two cans. Eight had already been opened, and half of the remaining cans contained octopuses of up to 35 centimetres (14 inches) from arm to arm. Doubtless the sea otter would be back again for canned octopus.

Incisors on both upper and lower jaws are used to wedge open shells, bite through urchin tests and scrape out shells. Large, flat molars grind and chew. When eating a large crab, for example, the otter holds the crab on its chest, ripping the legs off and chewing them one at a time. Then, holding the carapace, or top shell, in both paws, the otter uses its teeth to open the shell. The otter holds the crab shell like a large bowl against its mouth as it scrapes and licks out any remaining edible parts.

The same system is used for large urchins and abalone. Like any other part of an otter's foraging and feeding behaviour, the activity is brisk, efficient and energetic. For a not-so-large animal, a sea otter can put away a remarkable amount of seafood in one meal. For example, one otter ate twenty-four pismo clams (average 10 to 13 centimetres, or 4 to 5 inches) and two spiny mole crabs in two hours and fifteen minutes. Another ate fourteen large pismo clams and thirty-seven spiny mole crabs in four hours.

Although the sea otter grooms on and off all day, it does so most vigorously after a bout of diving and eating. The repeated rhythm of dive-collect-eat, dive-collect-eat, has lasted an hour or more. Now it is time for the otter to wash up, to scrub, lick and rinse every hair of its magnificent coat. Each bit of oil and debris will be washed away, as every centimetre of fur on every part of the otter's body is attacked with the same meticulous vigour. It is also time to restore the fur's depleted air layer. With each foraging dive, the sea otter loses more air from its fur. As it plunges deeper and deeper, air escapes in a mist of fine bubbles that follows the diving otter like a cloud of underwater dust. Just as any air-filled container released underwater rockets to the surface, so the layer of air trapped in the sea otter's fine underfur squeezes out between the guard hairs as the otter dives deeper, the water pressure increases, and the air fights to escape.

Air pressed out of the otter's fur will not automatically be replaced by a simple shrug and a shake. It must be painstakingly restored as the sea otter alternately rubs and lifts handfuls of fur to its mouth, first drying the fur and then blowing warm air back into it. The principle is the same as that of the hair dryer used by hairdressers to give temporary lift and fullness to a human head of hair. Eventually the reduced air blanket is brought back to the otter's satisfaction and it is time to rest.

The well-fed, well-groomed otter raises its large, furred hind flippers out of the water and arranges them one over the other across its abdomen. With head resting forward on its chest, the otter covers its eyes with its forepaws, hooks them behind its head as if to support its neck or simply holds its arms straight up, as if it were a surgeon waiting to receive sterile gloves. Now it closes its eyes and sleeps, absolutely still except for the slow sculling of its tail.

NEXT PAGE: *A healthy, unpolluted marine environment is essential to maintaining the sea otter's food supply.*

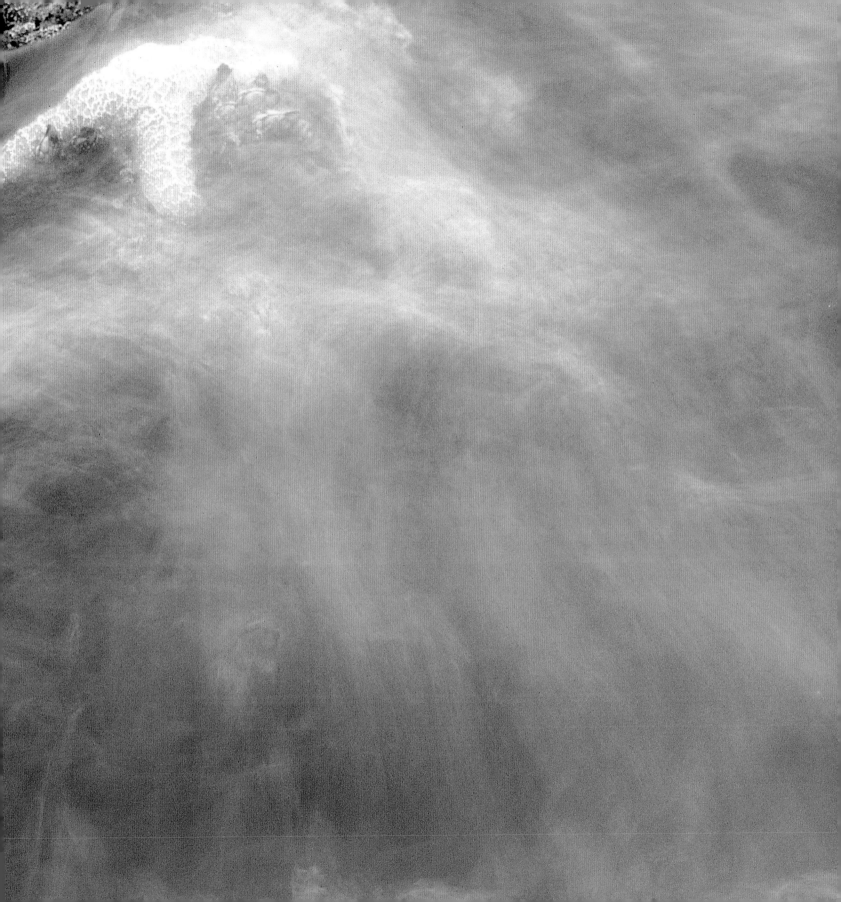

Powerful strokes of large hind flippers propel a sea otter to the sea floor to forage.

The sea otter's relish for abalone brings this efficient underwater hunter into conflict with abalone divers.

A sea otter always eats at the
surface, using its chest as a
lunch counter and a convenient
place to put its favourite rock
while eating.

In general, sea otters eat an
enormous variety of marine
animals, but as individuals they
often specialize in hunting three
or four species. This sea otter is
ready to enjoy a sea star.

41

When schools of opalescent squid come inshore to spawn, sea otters enjoy a temporary feast.

Sea otters collect small pink scallops underwater by tucking a half dozen or more of them into the loose skin folds under each arm, which act as handy shopping bags.

42

Brilliant sea stars become a sea otter's snack when the arm tips are bitten off so that soft parts can be sucked out.

The purple sea urchin is one of more than 160 food items consumed by sea otters.

43

Sensitive whiskers help the sea otter locate food at depths where light is dim.

The sea otter uses a rock as an anvil to break open hard-shelled clams.

44

*Underwater the sea otter uses a
rock for a hammer to dislodge a
large abalone.*

Cheeks and face are thoroughly washed and groomed after eating.

A sea otter wrapped in a
blanket of kelp.

With its sensitive forepaws, the
sea otter can search for snails
among the kelp fronds or pat
under rocks for limpets and
small crabs.

Lush kelp forests are home to the sea otter and to an entire community of marine organisms.

FACING PAGE: Small crabs, snails and other edible organisms are hiding in this mass of kelp.

Snails living on the kelp stipes are collected and eaten by sea otters.

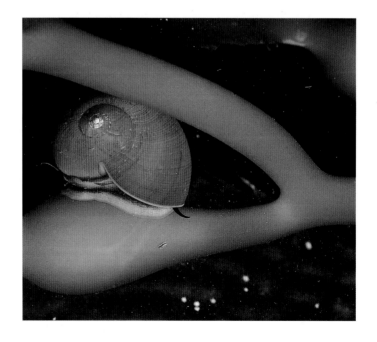

For thousands of years, sea otters and their prey existed in a kind of dynamic harmony. After the great fur hunt, when sea otters were for all practical purposes eliminated as predators on many invertebrate species, a new order developed on the sea floor. Studies of areas occupied by the sea otter over time suggest a sequence of events.

Sea otters in the Aleutian Islands were studied in the mid-1930s, when the population was small and the habitat was large. At that time, the otters were eating mostly sea urchins, suggesting that these were abundant and therefore quickly and easily harvested. The balance of the otters' diet consisted of mollusks. In total, in the 1930s and 1940s, sea otters at Amchitka were eating only a half dozen different species. Yet by the late 1960s, sea otters at the same place were eating forty-two different species, including a greater percentage of fish.

It is logical that the sea otter would eat the tastiest and most easily available food, particularly when the otter has the ability, range and dexterity to choose from a vast menu of items, as has been demonstrated in many studies and observations. As the most preferred food becomes less abundant, however, the animal will naturally turn to other, perhaps less preferred but more abundant species. For example, as it becomes more difficult to find large sea urchins, the sea otter may pursue crabs or chitons.

Another factor is what the prey are eating. As the urchins are eliminated, the food they were eating will now have a reprieve. Since the number of urchins grazing on the large kelps has been reduced, these plants can now flourish where previously they were eaten by urchins. With the growth of large kelp forests come the animals that live on the kelp, such as kelp crabs and a variety of snails. Now the snails, which are available and easy to catch, become prey of choice. One otter was seen to collect ten turban snails from the kelp canopy in less than sixty seconds. Fast food and no diving needed!

There is little doubt that sea otters have an effect on the abundance and variety of invertebrate species within their habitat. And there is no doubt that when sea otters harvest abalone, pismo clams or urchins, and human harvesters are after the same species, there simply are not going to be as many clams, urchins or abalones for people as there were before the sea otters arrived on the scene. Some people believe that the human species has exclusive rights to any resource and that human fishers should never have to share food with wildlife, much less defer to the needs of these animals. But the supply of shellfish is limited, and we are in competition with sea otters for it, just as we are in competition with seals for salmon. To some people, the solution is simple: eliminate the competition. Kill it, poison it, frighten it away, or capture it and take it somewhere else.

Other people acknowledge that the seals, sea otters and other animals were there first and that they are adapted to live where they do and eat what they do. These people believe that the animals should be left in peace and protected, since they have far fewer options than do the few people who harvest and eat abalone, for example.

These conflicts have been around for a long time and will not disappear, but they are likely to be absorbed in much broader issues involving habitats, ecosystems and the entire reassessment of resource use. The traditional line of thinking was that if people made a living by harvesting a certain resource, that was justification enough for eliminating the competition. Now there are those who believe that just because abalone divers make a living at harvesting abalones, this does not justify eliminating sea otters so that the otters' share of abalones is transferred to people.

Much effort has gone into determining what effect foraging sea otters have on the plant and animal life in the areas they occupy. Studies have been conducted comparing two similar habitats, one with otters and one without. In general, it has been found that when sea otters have been around for a while, the large grazers, such as abalone and sea urchins, are greatly reduced. In addition, there is a dramatic increase in the size and abundance of large kelps. Large kelps, or kelp forests, as they are frequently called, host a variety of animals, including juvenile fish of many species, which find protection in the kelp forest. It would be tempting to propose a simple and logical chain of events: introduce the sea otter, which reduces the abalone and urchin, and up springs the kelp, which then hosts a new abundance of kelp-dependent animals. This sequence of events may occur in some areas, but so little of the sea otter's range has escaped the impact of human activity that it is nearly impossible to separate the otter's effect on a habitat from other factors. Fishing, pollution, sewage outfalls, agricultural runoff and kelp harvesting are but a few such factors. In addition, natural events such as climatic change and ocean currents affect habitat, as do a host of other things we simply don't know about. We do know that in areas where otters are well established and appear to be at their peak numbers, the number of herbivorous invertebrates is reduced. Here a larger part of the sea otter's diet is fish, snails and kelp crabs, and sea otters spend more time looking for food than in areas where they are newcomers.

Conversely, in an area that is newly occupied by sea otters, there is an abundance of herbivorous invertebrates, such as sea urchins and abalone. In such areas, 100 per cent of the otter's diet is invertebrates, and significantly less time is spent foraging.

A young sea otter resting on shore during stormy weather may fall prey to a hungry coyote.

The sea otter is an efficient and hard-working predator. On this day, as on every other day, it has worked hard for its food. After it has eaten abundantly, groomed itself and found a protected resting place, it slips into a restoring sleep. While the otter sleeps, however, its predators do not. Everywhere, every day, life in the wild means that some animals eat and some animals are eaten. The sea otter is no exception. It is a predator, and it in turn is preyed upon. Predators of the sea otter are generally opportunists, ready to take advantage of the young, the inexperienced and those weakened by disease or severe weather.

A possible scenario might go something like this. A young male otter, less than a year old and recently separated from his mother, is en route to a new location. He is bold, he is energetic, and he is moving in response to some instinct that tells him to strike out on his own for a distant place. A few hours of steady swimming puts him well past familiar coves and inlets where he and his mother hunted together. He continues swimming into the early afternoon, when the sky darkens, the temperature drops, and the wind picks up. With startling speed, a spring storm whips the sea into a vicious, rolling boil. The youngster finds it hard to swim in the sloppy sea and searches without success for a sheltered spot. Finally, near midnight, the exhausted otter half-walks, half-crawls out of the water and over a small stretch of wave-soaked sand. There he collapses behind a large boulder, its massive head and shoulders rising above the sand and shielding him from the wind. Overcome with cold, hunger and fatigue, the otter sleeps.

By early morning, the storm is over and little evidence of its brutal hand remains. A spent moon sinks, pulled towards the horizon with the outgoing tide. In the dirty grey dawn, as the young otter sleeps on, an older, more experienced land-dwelling animal pads ever so quietly on the rocks above. The coyote pricks his large, pointed ears, which make instant, minute adjustments. His body freezes. Only his darting eyes betray any movement. Suddenly the coyote charges, running full speed at the young otter. Now instantly awake, the otter is frantic to reach the water and safety. But the coyote is fast. The young sea otter is terrified and clumsy on the wet sand. Jaws close over the otter's head, and its short life ends with the sound of a breaking bone.

Terrestrial predators like the coyote need a particular set of circumstances to catch a sea otter. The otter must be on land, it cannot be too large, and it must be ambushed before it can escape to the water. Airborne predators need a different set of circumstances to ensure success.

This scenario takes place in the spring in the Far North, somewhere in Alaska, perhaps. With milder weather and longer days, spring in the North is a time of rebirth and renewal, on land, in the sea and in the air. Everywhere there is evidence of new life, as grasses and flowers burst forth and newborn animals appear. Just off shore in a beautiful sheltered cove surrounded by steep, forest-covered banks, a group of mother sea otters raft peacefully together with their newborn pups curled sleeping on their chests. One mother sinks silently from under her pup so as not to waken it. She leaves it floating like a downy loaf of bread on the water's surface as she rolls forward and dives to the sea floor to forage. She quickly moves between lush, seaweed-covered boulders, looking for crabs tiptoeing from one rock to the other.

Above her, another mother on the surface accidentally bumps the sleeping pup, awakening him. Startled and alone, he shrieks his piercing baby cry, guaranteed to bring his mother instantly. But below water, she cannot hear him. High on a naked snag, another mother hears and sees the untended infant. The eagle mother—her head draped in a hood of white feathers, revealing only intense black eyes and a huge, hooked beak—is majestic and alert on her nest. She makes no unnecessary movements. With herself and her two demanding chicks to feed, the eagle cannot afford to waste a single calorie. With eyes riveted on the sea otter pup, she pushes off from the nest in powerful flight, dropping precisely onto the crying pup. Talons extended, she scoops it off the water in a smooth, perfect pass.

It has been less than a minute since the sea otter mother dove to find food, but her pup is gone. She listens for his cry and does not hear it. She searches and sniffs among the other pups, looking for her own, but she does not find it. She will continue to look for some days, and if during this time she finds a pup without a mother, she will adopt it and care for it as if it were her own, so strong is the maternal instinct in the female sea otter.

The coyote and the eagle prey on the young and the very young. The coyote, not a large animal itself, would have difficulty killing a full-grown otter. The eagle is limited by how much weight it can carry; consequently, a pup much over a week or two old will be safe from predation, since it will be too heavy for the eagle to lift.

There is one predator, however, from which no sea otter can escape, no matter what its size. It is the most terrifying predator in the sea—the great white shark.

The great white prowls temperate coastal waters throughout the world. Over 3 metres (10 feet) long, it is also surprisingly thick bodied. Massive muscles propel its bulk and power its head and jaws. With its great shearing teeth, like a mouthful of razors, it carves off chunks of animals much larger than itself. Nothing in the ocean is safe from attack, including the sea otter.

Shark-lacerated sea otter carcasses found on beaches in California, most often near Big Sur and north, are chilling testimony to the presence of the great white and its efficiency as a killer. There is a mystery, though, and that is, why don't the sharks eat the otters? A mortally wounded sea otter could never escape a shark. Is it a case of mistaken identity? Great whites in the vicinity prey heavily on young elephant seals and harbour seals, making one great slashing attack from beneath and behind their prey and then hanging back until the victim bleeds to death before consuming it. Could it be that sea otters float when dead and seals sink? Could it be that the shark is not programmed to take a dead animal from the surface? Or are the beached carcasses simply leftovers after an unknown number of sea otters have been eaten? Unquestionably, great white shark attacks are a cause of death in California sea otters and perhaps in sea otters farther north, but are sea otters specifically targeted prey? This question has yet to be answered.

A *newborn sea otter left untended at the surface while its mother dives for food is easy prey for a bald eagle.*

CHAPTER 3

Life Cycle of the Sea Otter

One day in mid-January when I was working at the Vancouver Aquarium, two visitors from Sealand in Victoria were in my office. As our visit was drawing to a natural close, I suggested we all take a stroll through the aquarium's public areas and have a look at the sea otters. They were outside, and on this winter day the wet grey concrete underfoot and on the walls melted monotonously with the wet grey sky. The exhibit was like a large room. One wall was glass, offering a full view, both above and below water. The other three walls had been transformed into rocky cliffs, ledges and overhangs to give an impression of the animal's natural habitat. The pool bottom was also irregular, with boulder outcroppings and underwater bays. Natural algae grew in soft mats on the underwater surfaces and swayed in the constantly circulating current.

As we rounded the corner of the exhibit, a single glance placed all three adult otters —two females, one male—in the pool. The same glance registered an impression of something different. Looking more carefully, I could see an otter working vigorously with a large handful of wet fur. With profound amazement, I realized one of the females had given birth. We hadn't even known she was pregnant!

Now the three of us strained our eyes in the fading light to watch the dark brown animal in the black water, trying to take in every aspect of the moment. The fur ball in the female's paws was very small and very wet, obviously newly delivered. It was also lifeless and floppy.

To say the mother tended to her newborn would not properly describe her activity. She *worked* on it, vigorously and none too gently, licking it, rolling it over, its tiny hind flippers flapping this way and that like tiny wet dishrags. She cleaned the lifeless little thing over and over again. She chewed at the fur, scrubbed it and blew on it without stopping. She was not exactly anxious, but she was definitely focused, intent and very, very busy.

A mother sea otter grooms her youngster.

61

The pup was so small—hardly bigger than a rat—that the mother could contain the object of her labours between her chin and two forepaws as she floated on her back in the water, lifting it and rolling it over in her paws again and again. At last a downy ball began to emerge from the sack of wet fur. I thought I saw movement and felt a painful pinch of hope in my chest. Then, as the mother was carried by the current in front of the window where I stood watching, I saw it. A tiny blue, blue eye was open in the fluffy ball. The pup was alive! I had never seen a newborn sea otter before. It was so little, so completely helpless, but it was alive.

A half hour had passed. Grooming the pup continued without interruption for another hour. By then it was a perfectly dry, fluffy ball of soft brown. The mother fitted her treasure high on her chest under her chin, and folding her forearms securely around her newborn, she rested for the first time. It was now nearly six o'clock, and there was no light left. We slipped away, leaving the mother and her babe to their first night together, feeling enormously privileged for having been able to watch the first precious moments in this sea otter's life. Later, reflecting on the afternoon's events, I realized that in the wild initial grooming would be a matter of life and death for a newborn otter. With no fat for thermal insulation, the wet baby would quickly chill and die if its mother didn't groom and dry its fur, providing her little one with its first baby blanket. No wonder she worked so hard at grooming her baby's fur; she was racing against time. Imagine the hazards facing a newborn otter in the windy, northern seas as each gust of wind saps what little body heat the animal might be able to generate. If a dry coat is essential to an adult, it is even more critical to a new pup.

I also wondered during that first night how normal the aquarium pup was. It was so feeble that I thought it might be premature. How would it ever suckle?

My observations of mother and pup resumed at first light the following morning. The youngster lay on its mother's ample chest as it had been placed, without adding any of its own nestling down movements. Early attempts to raise its head resulted in a wobbly half arc before the little head flopped down. Sometimes I could see random movements of little furry hind flippers.

The nursing mystery was quickly solved. The mother sea otter simply lifted the pup up and turned it around, accurately placing the pup's head at her abdominal nipples. The pup did not have to search at all. While the pup suckled, the mother groomed the pup's hind quarters. During the early weeks, the mother sea otter nursed her pup irregularly, anywhere from one to eight minutes at ten- to forty-minute intervals.

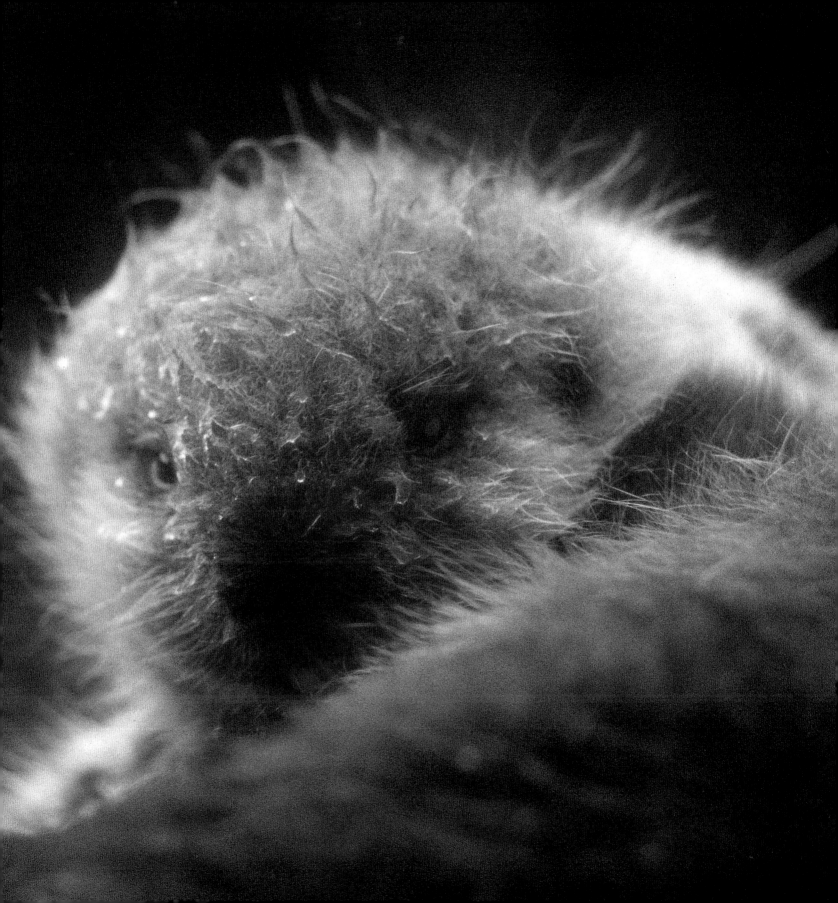

A single helpless pup is born in
the water. With no nest or den to
protect her offspring, the mother
sea otter cradles her newborn on
her chest.

Like helpless newborns of many species, this one spent most of its time sleeping for the first two weeks. It slept soundly while its mother swam on her back or groomed herself. It slept soundly as she vigorously groomed it. It slept soundly as she gently slid it off her chest to float beside her in the water while she groomed herself or dove for food. The pup slept soundly as she deftly placed it back on her chest when she finished grooming. It never even knew it had its first float in the water. Soon the pup was sleeping sea otter style on its back, not in the water but on its mother's chest. When a tiny arc of urine sailed over the rotund little abdomen, we knew the pup was a male.

The pup developed quickly, loosing its wobbly neck and gaining in strength and coordination. Within weeks it sat up on its mother's chest while she slept for a change. By now he could crawl around on the living platform of his mother's chest, where it was always dry and warm. Her chest was first a cradle and now a playpen. Scrubbing his face with tiny paws, he demonstrated his first attempts at grooming. His face was changing from a powder puff with two eyes into one that had real expression, with a black nose, short, bushy whiskers and a trim mouth. His colour was darkening to the most magnificent deep, rich brown, which contrasted with the bubble-gum pink of his mouth and with his tiny white teeth.

The great advantage in observing the behaviour of a captive-born arrival is that its activities both above and below water can be recorded in great detail. There is always the question, though, as to how accurately behaviour in captivity reflects "natural" behaviour in the wild. Fortunately, observers using shore-based spotting scopes have observed a few births and a number of pups in the wild. The observations from these studies are consistent with the data from otters in captivity and provide a good picture of early development and behaviour in the sea otter.

Females do not reveal their pregnancy by any outward appearance. The only indication of a pending birth in the aquarium was reduced appetite the day before delivery, but even this is not absolute. Pregnancy is very hard to determine by outward appearance, since an otter's coat is usually too large for its frame and is very loose. Out of water, the heavy fur hangs, and as it drys with a shake, it is nearly impossible to tell if a female has gained any weight.

Birth typically takes place in the water and is very quick. During delivery, the female rolls in somersault fashion, as she would normally do when grooming her tail, hind flippers or rump. On one roll, she emerges with a small, wet pup in her teeth.

There are reports that birth occurs on land as well. Birth, like eating, is a messy affair, and one would think that the otter would be able to clean up after delivery faster and better in water than on land. Certainly a female with a newborn will haul out onto land carrying her youngster in her mouth. She will settle herself in the identical position she would assume in the water—in a reclining position, her back against a boulder with her newborn snuggled high on her chest.

Newborn sea otters range in weight from about 1.4 to 2.3 kilograms (3 to 5 pounds). There is typically one offspring per pregnancy, and if there are twins, which is rare, the mother can only successfully rear one. Although a mother may try to rear both, she soon abandons one and cares for the other. Unlike the river otter, which has a land-based den in which the female can safely leave her litter while she goes off to find food, the sea otter mother is herself her baby's nest and cradle and its only protection from the killing chill of the ocean until the pup has developed the fur coat and minimum body mass needed for survival in water. In addition, a mother sea otter would be hard-pressed to feed more than one extra mouth. Her own food requirements are large, and the burden of even one fast-growing offspring is significant.

The season of birth varies geographically. In Alaska, for example, or the Near Islands in the Aleutian chain, the majority of pups are born in the early spring. Violent winter storms are challenging enough for adults, but with choppy seas constantly slopping over a mother sea otter's chest, a newborn would be constantly wet, making it difficult for the pup to suckle or even sleep. Milder summer weather is easier on the young, and it also means that females can disperse out of coastal inlets and coves where they have spent the winter and move into distant shallows in open water, where food is probably more abundant and more accessible. As well, females and young would be farther away from coyotes, which patrol the shallows for young pups, and eagles, which readily take unattended newborn sea otters as food for their own hungry nestlings. In California, at the opposite end of the sea otter's range, pupping occurs in reverse. Here, though pups are seen year round, the largest number are born from January to March.

Mother sea otters are extraordinarily protective of their young. When danger threatens, the female with a very young pup takes her pup in her teeth, like a female dog with a puppy, and dives in an attempt to flee the danger. The greater hazard is that if the mother is forced to make repeated dives, she can drown her pup. The tiny lungs simply can't keep up with the repeated dives. For this reason, otter watching from boats or kayaks should be done with extreme care. Mothers and young should not be approached.

Even when pups are older and quite adept at diving on their own, an anxious mother will forcibly grasp her youngster, its back against her chest, and cross her forearms over the shoulders and across the chest of her young. She dives out of sight with her youngster, who typically shrieks in protest, but to no avail.

True babyhood is short for a sea otter pup but labour intensive for its mother. She devotes fully 25 to 30 per cent of her waking hours tending to this little creature, grooming and feeding it, while still needing to groom herself, forage for herself, travel to and from feeding areas, and get some rest.

NEXT PAGE: *Once a pup is too heavy to lie on its mother's chest, it floats at a right angle to her while it suckles.*

A young sea otter rides, plays
and feeds on the furry platform
of its mother's chest, where it
keeps warm and dry.

Females with large, dependent pups must hunt extra-hard to have enough food to share.

FROM PUP TO YOUNGSTER IN A FEW SHORT WEEKS

The passive, cuddly newborn becomes a full-blown toddler at about four weeks. Now when it is left floating at the surface while its mother dives, the youngster makes vigorous if fruitless attempts to swim. It rolls onto its chest and makes great undulating exertions in an attempt to dive. The result is a miniature Ogopogo lurching caterpillar-like across the surface, bumping into any object in the path. The youngster is too buoyant to dive, but rolling over onto its belly at the water's surface, it peers underwater and watches its mother's progress as she swims deeper and deeper.

Within a few weeks, junior is swimming and diving with his mother, grooming himself and looking and behaving like a miniature sea otter. Although he is eating solid food (his mother has been offering him pieces of hers since he was a few weeks old), which he actively solicits from his mother, he still suckles regularly. He is too large to climb onto her chest now, so he drapes himself crosswise, his head resting on her abdomen; together mother and thriving youngster form the shape of a *T*. In the early months of diving, the young otter is unlikely to collect much that is useful. Accompanying his mother on foraging dives is a time to learn, to develop diving skills and endurance, and to just explore.

As the young sea otter grows, the bond between mother and pup remains extremely strong and physical contact is constant. When the pup is awake, it constantly plays with its mother. It climbs all over her body and head and plays with her flippers, her paws, her face. Touching, grooming and embracing continue. Even females without pups are very tactile and hold each other if frightened or uncertain.

When it is time to nap, the mother wraps her arm around the pup's neck in a half-Nelson-style wrestling hold, or they hold hands to keep from drifting apart while they are sleeping. Since sea otters always sleep on their backs, it is quite comfortable for a mother to hold her youngster's paw between her own as they snooze. One or both animals may wrap themselves in strands of kelp when it is available. Since the kelp is securely attached to the ocean floor, it makes a convenient anchor line.

No portrait of a young sea otter would be complete without a description of its vocal behaviour. Very early in life, sea otter pups emit a most piercing shriek. The first time is usually when the otter discovers it has been abandoned at the surface while its mother goes hunting. Little wonder that mothers wait for their youngsters to fall asleep before rolling them into the water.

As the pup becomes more active, it learns to scream for everything it wants or doesn't want: food, attention, play, companionship, being taken on a dive or being separated from a playmate. The demanding scream carries over distances and rises above other sounds. In the aquarium, screaming pups could be heard far off in the parking lot above the sounds of children shouting or bus engines and other mechanical noises. The scream is effective, since mothers respond instantly. Observations in the field demonstrate the scream's survival value; it can be heard above the sound of wind and crashing surf and helps mothers to find their youngsters in noisy, active seas. A sea otter pup is a very small item in great rolling swells, and mother and pup may become visually separated by large waves when she goes on a foraging dive.

Most sea otters are sociable, if not social. They tend to congregate in groups known as rafts, which are typically composed of either one sex or the other. When females group together, there will be a large number of pups together. Consequently, the pups will have playmates. They enjoy the rough and tumble of water play, but mothers are ever vigilant and quick to haul a pup away if they think things are getting out of hand.

Over the years, I have had the opportunity to watch the growth and behaviour of many young sea otters born in captivity, and as can be expected there is considerable variation in temperament, behaviour and development. Nevertheless, there is a behavioural trend in young otters that I believe is characteristic of the species and may have significant survival value in the wild. Sea otter juveniles are not simply "energetic"; in human terms, we would describe such youngsters as "a handful," or even juvenile delinquents. It is particularly noticeable when two or more are together. Their energy level is phenomenal, their appetites prodigious and their curiosity insatiable. Any moveable object is used to bash, crush and dismantle. They can climb. They are escape artists; they are furniture movers. They will destroy anything they can put their paws on by chewing, pushing, pulling or lifting. They will undo bolts, lift extremely heavy grates underwater and unlace boots. They touch, taste, smell and thoroughly examine everything within their reach. Their restlessness is boundless, and even vigorous bouts of tumbling play with other youngsters, or harassing their mothers, don't seem to tire them out.

High energy is a characteristic of many young mammals and probably helps less experienced animals find enough food, sheer effort substituting for skill and efficiency. As an adult, the sea otter has a particularly large challenge before it, since it must find up to 25 per cent of its body weight in food every day. An individual with energy and an investigative, persistent nature will be more successful in finding new food items and harvesting techniques than an individual that is less creative. An example of such an investigative individual is the young otter in Monterey Bay who learned how to harvest small octopuses living in discarded soft drink cans at the bottom of the bay. Tool use and clam digging are part of this behavioural trait also.

A mother sea otter's devotion to her pup is legendary.

For the first few weeks after birth, when the pup is too small to dive with its mother, it is left to float alone at the water's surface while she quickly dives and returns.

Juvenile sea otters will happily
play with anything or anybody,
including a human diver.

Older pups have an insatiable
curiosity. Here a youngster has
found a wonderful new toy, a
piece of plywood floating in the
kelp.

Soon the juvenile sea otter will leave its mother, its young companions and the security of the group.

Young sea otters engage in lots of rough and tumble play when mothers and pups raft together after feeding.

For a young otter of five or six months of age, life is sweet, rich and full. Then one day a large male appears. He cruises through the raft of females, approaching each one and sniffing her hind quarters. A female may snap, hiss and slap the male on the face with her hind flipper. Rejection is quick and final. There is no mistaking the message.

When the big male approaches a large pup's mother, she does not snap or rebuff the male's advances. The pup's mother and the male move off to the edge of the raft, ignoring the pup completely. Alarmed and rejected, the pup shrieks in protest and tries to climb onto his mother. His mother, who has doted on him all these months, doesn't seem to hear his cries. Despite the pup's attempts at interference, the two adults ignore him. They don't try to push him away or shut him up; they simply act as if he doesn't exist. The pup doesn't understand that his mother is ready to mate.

The term "courtship" cannot be applied to the mating rituals of sea otters. There are few preliminaries, and acceptance in the female is more of a lack of rejection. If you have ever observed sea otters mating, you will fully understand why the females show so little enthusiasm.

Copulation in sea otters is often a violent and disfiguring affair. The male grabs the female from behind and then clamps his large jaws onto her head, neck or nose and upper jaw. Teeth that do such an efficient job on urchins, crabs and abalones have a similar effect on the female's nose. As the pair rolls and thrashes, the female is held underwater most of the time. With her nose covered and her mouth pulled open, she can hardly breath. The first time I observed this, I was sure the female would drown. Brief glimpses of her wide-open bloodshot eyes didn't help.

Mating can last for a few minutes or up to twenty minutes. When it is over, the female emerges with a shredded and bleeding nose. Although it heals, she will be scarred for life. Older, more experienced males tend to have briefer, less violent encounters with females. Still, there is no way mating in sea otters could ever be described as romantic!

A mated pair may copulate on and off and stay together for up to three days. Once pairing is over, it is truly over. If the female has a large pup, life resumes as before. Even if she doesn't, she has no further relationship with her future offspring's sire. A male sea otter's role in the reproductive process begins and ends with copulation.

A female can give birth in as little as five months. Some investigators believe that the gestation period is four months. Others believe that there is a period of delayed implan-

A torn and bloodied nose
identifies this sea otter as a
recently mated female.

tation (a time when the fertilized egg remains alive in the mother but does not begin active development) for four months or so followed by an active pregnancy of similar duration, for a total of eight or nine months. The period of delayed implantation may vary.

In any case, under optimum conditions, female sea otters can give birth annually, producing perhaps eight, ten or even more pups in a lifetime. How many actually do have a pup every year is not known. Perhaps where food is abundant, environmental conditions are good, and females are in their prime, they do pup every year. This may explain how sea otters in new areas, such as the coasts of southeastern Alaska and British Columbia, have increased their numbers so dramatically in a relatively short period of time.

In general, however, females are likely to produce less than one pup a year. Five or six pups per female is probably a more realistic number, and of these not all would be expected to survive to maturity. Sea otters, like all wild animals, over-reproduce to allow for losses through disease, predation and accidents.

THE LIFE CYCLE CONTINUES

For most mammals, there comes a time when the youngster must leave its mother and make its own way. In sea otters, this occurs between five and eight months of age. The female may initiate early weaning if food is in short supply. Later weaning, at eight months, for example, could be more beneficial to the pup. By now the pup is more correctly referred to as a juvenile or a subadult. At eight months, the young otter is as large as its mother or nearly so, and it has had the benefit of watching an experienced hunter obtain food. It is time to try living independently.

At this time, the young otter's desire to be beside its mother is replaced by a restlessness and a desire to strike out on its own. A young male may travel over 100 kilometres (62 miles) before joining a group of young males. In a few years, another powerful urge will drive the young adult male to search for a female. Some years later, when he is eight or nine years old and in his prime, he may become a territorial male, with a section of shoreline to patrol and a raft or two of females to mate with. A female will likely reach sexual maturity at age three and have her first pup at age four or five. And so the cycle continues.

In the closing decade of the twentieth century, there is a good chance that a young otter will reach full maturity and live to produce many offspring, even though it faces perils unique to the age in which it lives. The contemporary sea otter lives with all the traditional dangers of weather, predators and disease as well as the contemporary hazards of pollution, fishing nets or traps and conflicts with seafood harvesters. Nevertheless, the sea otter's future is full of opportunity and promise.

The young sea otter is equipped with remarkable physical attributes: strength, stamina, a marvellous coat and well-tuned sensory abilities, to name a few. The otter is alert, observant, energetic and resolute. This is its natural history, a story of superb adaptation to a demanding environment.

But the sea otter has another history, the story of what happened when its home on the islands of the Aleutian chain was discovered $2^1/2$ centuries ago. Our young sea otter, swimming alone and determined towards a destination it has never seen, is not aware of any past but its own. The otter does not know that being alive on the first day of its independence is a miracle, given the events of the past. It does not know about the reign of terror that lasted nearly a century and almost exterminated the sea otter forever.

NEXT PAGE: *When less than a year old, a young otter will strike out on its own, often travelling far away from where it was born and raised.*

88

PART II

At the Hands of Humans

CHAPTER 4

The Great Hunt

It is the fourth of November, 1741, in the northwest corner of the Pacific Ocean. Winds of 145 kilometres (90 miles) an hour shriek over tiny, treeless islands, and mountainous waves, some 12 metres (40 feet) high, pound the islands' rocky shores. A little wooden ship, barely 24.5 metres (80 feet) long, is floundering in the wind, waves and fog. Its ice-covered sails are split. There are no sailors on deck, so violent is the storm. A dozen of the crew have died; the rest, sick and weak from scurvy, are terrified in the face of such fury. As the unmanned ship is swept in ugly lurches towards exposed rocks, a giant wave picks up the vessel and carries it over the jagged reef into a lagoon. Suddenly all is quiet. The ravaged ship sits painfully beaten but calm, in quiet water.

Christened the *St. Peter* and commanded by Captain Vitus Jonassen Bering in the service of Russia, the ship will never sail again. After five difficult months at sea, it has been wrecked on an unnamed island somewhere east of Kamchatka. Fortunately for the shipwrecked crew, Georg Wilhelm Steller, a botanist, biologist and student of medicine, is on board. Steller knows how to treat scurvy using medicinal plants dug from the harsh Aleutian landscape. He is also the one who prowls the island looking for animals that can be killed for food. In protected bays and inlets, he finds smallish brown animals floating on their backs in the near-shore swells. Steller knows these animals as the Kamchatka sea beaver. Today we call them sea otters.

The island, which would later be named Bering Island for the expedition's captain, was uninhabited. As a result, none of its wildlife, including the sea otter, had ever been hunted. The sea otters were not frightened by Steller's presence and were easily killed. Thus, the sea otter became the staple food for the crew. The animals had little fat and the meat was tough and stringy, but it was fresh food. In addition, the furred skins were incredibly dense and warm. Nature provided well for the sailors; abandoned fox holes

Aleut hunters pursued the sea otters in their fast and highly manoeuvrable skin boats.
PAINTING BY EMILIE CURTIS

were enlarged for shelter from wind and snow, plants kept scurvy at bay, and sea otters provided food and coverings.

As the dreary winter dragged on, the bored seamen turned to gambling for entertainment. To stay in the game, a player needed a stake, and after any valuable possessions had been gambled away, a new form of currency was needed. Sea otter skins became that new currency. In spite of Steller's protestations, animals were killed for no other reason than to hoard their skins—an ugly murmur of things to come

Finally the winter passed. The snow melted and the seamen could begin building a new ship that would take them off the cold and barren island. A new vessel, built with materials salvaged from the wrecked ship, was less than half the length of the original *St. Peter*. It was dangerously small for the number of men it had to carry, but it was their only possible escape. The new boat was finally completed and ready to sail on 13 August 1742. Time was running out, not only because another winter was just around the corner, but also because food was increasingly difficult to get. After months of intensive hunting, the nearby sea otter herd was cautious and secretive. The otters no longer hauled out on shore to sleep, and in the water they were ever alert to the sound or smell of hunters. Steller wrote in his journal that more than nine hundred sea otters had been killed during the crew's eight months on the island.

The new ship left Bering Island with forty-six survivors, a supply of sea otter meat for the journey, and hundreds and hundreds of sea otter pelts stuffed into every possible space on the impossibly crowded little vessel. Two weeks later, the ship sailed into Avacha Bay. The sailors were home.

The arrival of the lustrous sea otter furs caused a sensation. Although rare, sea otter pelts were not an unknown item. Russian hunters, or *promyshleniki*, hunted sea otters in the spring in the Kuril Islands south of Kamchatka to sell to the Chinese. But this was a labour-intensive and dangerous proposition requiring a boat with six oarsmen and a hunter. The prospect of new and abundant sources of something as valuable as the "Kamchatka sea beaver" had the most ambitious fur hunters drooling in anticipation as they plotted how to get to the new hunting grounds first.

In the spring of 1743, Emilian Bassof, a military man, in partnership with a merchant, set off for Bering Island in a not-very-well-crafted boat, without aid of maps, navigational tools or experience. Remarkably, Bassof made it to Bering Island and visited another island close by. He spent the winter on the islands and returned intact the following summer with a handsome cargo of furs: sixteen hundred sea otters, two thousand blue foxes and two thousand fur seals. Even more remarkable is that Bassof made a repeat trip the following year, turning an even greater profit on that trip.

The great fur hunt was on. Boats of every description were constructed, many in such haste that they sank while still in sight of land. An unknown number of men drowned when their ships flew apart in violent storms, or starved to death on some piece of rock after a shipwreck. Some reached the islands to slaughter every animal they could find. And some returned home with a wealth of furs.

At first the ships headed for the Commander Islands, the group of islands, including Bering Island, named in honour of the Captain Commander, Vitus Bering. By 1745, however, the ships were beginning to cross the open expanse of the Bering Sea to the Aleutian chain.

NATIVE HUNTERS

Things changed dramatically when the *promyshleniki* moved away from Bering Island and invaded the Aleutian chain. These islands were inhabited. When the first ship landed and the inhabitants approached the intruders, the Russians could see that they were wearing long, shirt-like garments made of sea otter fur or bird feathers. Because the otters there had been hunted for centuries by the island's native people for food or clothing, they could not be clubbed on land as the Bering Island otters could. If the wily sea otters sensed a human anywhere, they stayed in the water, out of the hunter's reach. Pathetically clumsy on land, the animals were extraordinarily quick and agile in the water. The Russian hunters tried to chase the otters in the reef-filled water with the landing boats off their ship, but at the slightest disturbance the otters dove to safety. Even guns were no use. The *promyshleniki*, so bold and arrogant on land, were bumbling and impotent on the water.

At first the Russians traded what few items they had on board their ship for available pelts. The native people, later known as the Aleuts, traded what furs they had, but it wasn't very much; they had no reason to stockpile furs.

Frustration ran high among the Russian hunters. They were there to get as many sea otter pelts as they could, by whatever means and in as short a time as possible. They wanted the skin of every animal they could see, and they would stop at nothing, including hostage taking, enslavement and murder.

Through a long, bitter winter, Bering's shipwrecked crew had learned how difficult it was to survive on these cold and barren islands. Yet here was a group of strong, healthy

This native chief at Nootka
Sound, April 1778, is carrying
an arrowcase made of sea otter
skin. Drawing by John Webber.
PEABODY MUSEUM,
HARVARD UNIVERSITY.
PHOTOGRAPH BY HILLEL
BURGER.

people, thriving in an environment with virtually no land-based resources. How did they do it? The Aleuts had wonderful little boats, which the Russians called *baidarkas*, that were marvels of engineering, efficiency and ingenuity in the use of available materials. Since the wind-torn Aleutian Islands had virtually no trees, there was no wood for boats.Instead, the *baidarkas* were made of sea lion skin stretched tightly over a frame. Wood for the frame and ribs was carefully scavenged from driftwood and the small, twisted alders found on the island. At about 6 metres (20 feet) long and only 13.5 kilograms (30 pounds), the skin canoe was very light but also very fragile. The outer skin wrapped the bottom, sides and top of the vessel, with a hole the diameter of the paddler's body through which he could slip himself into the craft. The *baidarka* was barely as wide as a man's hips and not much deeper, meaning that a paddler sat flat on the boat bottom, legs and feet straight out in front. Hunting boats were generally designed for two men, one to handle the canoe with a double-bladed paddle while the other threw a spear at the quarry, which might be a fish, a sea lion, a seal or a sea otter. In the hands of an experienced Aleut, the *baidarka* was swift, silent, highly manoeuvrable and seaworthy. It could go anywhere and hunt anything in the sea.

It was clear that the *promyshleniki* needed the native people, with their superior knowledge and skill, to hunt the sea otters for them. When the Aleuts resisted, some were shot, and women, children or important community members were taken hostage to ensure compliance. They were subjected to the most savage blackmail; a hunter was required to produce a certain number of sea otter pelts to ensure the life of his wife or child. To resist meant torture or death as an example to others. No act was too brutal in the subjugation of the Aleuts, as the *promyshleniki* turned them into virtual slaves, forcing them to hunt sea otters. This became a pattern repeated in village after village as the rapacious fur hunters moved ever eastward through the Aleutian Islands and onto the northern mainland of North America.

Baidarkas travelled in groups to hunt the little sea otter, moving in on an otter raft with great speed and stealth. Sometimes the hunters would go out near the end of a storm, when the exhausted sea otters were asleep with their heads tucked under matted kelp fronds to keep the stinging rain or sleet out of their faces. Many sleeping otters could be clubbed and killed before one would waken and alarm the rest. Dead otters were skinned right at the boat with a single cut across the lower back and another cut down each hind leg. The pelt was heavy but loose, and it peeled off the carcass like a sock off a foot. The hunter then unlaced the waist piece on the canoe and stuffed the bloody pelt into the boat, kicking it forward as best he could so as not to lose a moment in killing more and more and more sea otters for the slave masters.

At other times, the hunters would find and surround a single animal. They would follow the otter's telltale trail of bubbles and force it to dive again and again, never giving it time to take a full breath. Eventually the terrorized otter's lungs would scream for air, and the animal would be forced to surface. Life-giving air would fill its lungs. Seconds later, a lance wound in the otter's neck would fill its lungs with its own warm blood.

The bloody pelt stuffed into the nose of a skin canoe was destined to make a long and hazardous journey back across the Pacific to Kamchatka, then overland 4800 kilometres (3,000 miles) west to the trading town of Kiakhta on the border of northern China. Here Chinese merchants would trade silks, teas, pearls and other treasures for the best pelts.

These in turn would be sold to wealthy Chinese mandarins who coveted the fine fur for elegant capes and decoration and trim on their elaborate gowns. The Russians then travelled to cities such as St. Petersburg and sold their exotic wares for fabulous sums. The demand for sea otter furs was unending, and so, it seemed, was the supply.

Sea otter were exterminated on Bering Island a short fifteen years after the Russians discovered them. But there were always more otters on the next island, and the hunters always found them. The contented, bewhiskered otters would gaze curiously over the tangled kelp and blue water at the huge, winged ships, never suspecting that they were about to die. And so the Russian fur traders moved across the Pacific, leaving a trail of death.

Sea otters were killed by the tens of thousands. So were other fur-bearing animals. Ship records show that the brothers Panof returned from the hunting grounds with a cargo of 5,000 sea otter and 1,100 red fox pelts. Ivan Popof, on his second trip, is recorded as bringing in 3,000 sea otters, 1,663 black foxes, 1,162 blue foxes, 1,025 red foxes and 230 cross foxes. In 1758, on Umiak Island, one vessel recorded 1,465 sea otters, 1,002 black foxes, 1,100 cross foxes, 400 red foxes and 58 blue foxes. With this level of destruction, prey species disappeared fast, forcing the hunters and their ships to move on to the next island and the next in a steady eastward movement through the seven hundred islands of the Aleutian chain. Within twenty years of Bering's expedition, the killer ships had covered three-quarters of the distance between Bering Island and Alaska. Sea otters were hunted year round. Unlike most other fur bearers, sea otters do not have a time of moult. Thus, the pelts were always prime. The sea was red with blood.

But the sea otters were not the only casualties of the hunt. The Aleuts' culture was destroyed, along with thousands of natives. Disease spread. Ships were wrecked with fortunes' worth of sea otter pelts on board. Everywhere there was death, destruction and disaster. Still the hunt went on. For every ship that went down, three more came out of Kamchatka. For every island that was killed clean of sea otters, there was another island on the horizon.

By 1768 or thereabouts, the hunting ships ran out of islands and reached Alaska.

A New Discovery, Another Hunt

For thirty years, the sea otter hunt belonged to the Russians. Then, in 1776, Captain James Cook, one of history's greatest navigators and explorers, left England and sailed to the North Pacific Ocean to search for the elusive Northwest Passage. He had made two previous voyages to the Pacific between 1769 and 1775, and these remarkable expeditions had stirred new interest in the search for a Northwest Passage to China. On a Sunday in late March of 1778, Cook's two vessels, the *Resolution*, under his command, and the *Discovery*, under Captain Clarke, sailed into a large bay on the west coast of what is now Vancouver Island. Large wooden canoes filled with native people approached the ships and made it clear that they were prepared to trade. Among the skulls and human hands offered for exchange were beautifully soft furs. Some were whole pelts; others were made into clothing, such as the long capes worn by high-status individuals. Neither Cook nor his men had ever seen or heard of a sea otter and had no idea of the fur's great value to the native people or anyone else. All they knew was that it was wonderfully soft and warm and would no doubt be useful as they travelled north later in the season. A month later, with supplies of wood and water replenished, the two ships weighed anchor and left Nootka Sound for points north.

In his journal, Cook notes the frequency and abundance of sea otters on their route north. Without knowing it, Cook was following the coastal range of the sea otter, from what is now northern British Columbia and the islands of southeastern Alaska to Cook Inlet, Prince William Sound and the Alaska Peninsula. Had Cook headed west along the Aleutians instead of north into the Bering Sea up to the Bering Strait, he might have witnessed first-hand the brutal destruction of the sea otter. Cook saw none of it because he headed north according to his assignment, which was to map and explore. It was unlikely that Cook would see sea otters farther north, since a frozen sea is an impenetrable barrier to a sea otter. Hence, the otters tended to stay in the Aleutian Islands, where the water was warmed by the Kuroshio Current. No matter how cold the air temperature, the sea remained fluid.

As the summer faded into fall and the North Pacific weather closed in, Cook turned and retraced his path south. He then sailed out into the Pacific to spend the winter in Hawaii before resuming his northern explorations the following year. That winter Cook was killed by native people in Hawaii, and although he never returned to the North Pacific, his ships did return the following season to resume the search. No Northwest Passage was found, and after the second season, the two vessels headed home.

For the men aboard the *Resolution* and the *Discovery*, the stop in Nootka Sound two seasons before must have seemed a lifetime away. They had sailed uncharted waters, gone into the Arctic, lost their great captain in a bloody murder and recently buried his second in command. On their homeward journey, they had crossed the Pacific and now prepared to stop briefly in the Chinese port of Canton for supplies.

Canton in the late 1700s was a colourful, noisy, exciting place. As an international trading centre, it received goods, news and information from all over the world. Authorities in Canton did not allow international traders to stay there year round and restricted their operations to the trading season between November and May. For the rest of the year, the international traders established themselves just to the south of Canton in the Portuguese port of Macau. Both ports had their own word-of-mouth communication systems, a lively network of talk between officials, labourers, scoundrels, hustlers and traders.

Perhaps one of Cook's crewman had thrown an old otter-skin robe over his shoulders against an early morning chill, or maybe a sailor was airing out his bedding on deck in the sunshine. In any case, someone, perhaps a fur trader who had been dealing with the Siberian fur traders in northern China, saw the fur and recognized it as sea otter. Not only did the English seamen have no idea that the pelts had any special value, but after seeing so many sea otters while sailing up the west coast of North America, they had become indifferent to the furs they had at first thought were so lovely. Worn-out furs had been discarded or used as mattresses.

When word reached Macau that sea otter furs were on board English vessels in Canton, the merchants went wild. They swarmed over the ships offering astronomical sums for even the poorest scraps of fur, and any English seaman who owned whole, prime skins reaped a surprise fortune. Suddenly the sea otters were no longer a dim memory of interesting animals sleeping in the kelp or porpoising in the surf; they were a stake in a gold mine.

The potential fortune to be made in sea otter pelts was dutifully detailed in the account of the Cook voyage to the Pacific, published in 1784. It was not long before entrepreneurs in England, North America and Europe had trading ships on the way to Nootka Sound. Ships supplied with goods to trade with the indigenous peoples for furs spent a season on the coast, with stops at Nootka Sound and other native villages along the coast. Ships would then depart for the open Pacific, winter in the Hawaiian Islands and proceed to China, where the furs were traded for goods such as teas, silks, porcelain, pearls and opium. These would then be brought home and sold in Europe or on the American east coast. By 1792, it was getting crowded in Nootka Sound. There was the *Jefferson* from Boston, the *Margaret* from New York, the *Grace* from England and the *Solide* from Marseilles. The Spanish were there too, though on the north coast they were more interested in collecting souls than sea otter pelts.

Unlike the Russians operating to the north, the Europeans and Americans were traders first. They were not interested in colonization or making slaves of the native people. There was no need. In contrast to the Russians, the newcomers had brought quality trade goods of such variety and in such quantity that the native people were more than willing to go out and get the pelts in anticipation of the annual arrival of the traders. Since the native people did all the hunting, it is likely that many of the traders never actually saw a live sea otter.

More ships arriving on the coast meant stiffer competition between the trading ships for the furs. The native people were shrewd traders themselves and quickly responded to the increasing demand for pelts by getting more and better trade goods for their sea otter skins. Firearms and whiskey were added to the usual trade articles of beads, cloth and metal items. Hunting pressure on the sea otters increased. The ships kept coming, and so did the otter skins.

Russians continued to operate in the north, slowly exterminating the sea otter as they advanced down the coast in search of more and more skins. Europeans and Americans operating in the south were now moving farther and farther north in search of the same thing. Eventually the two must meet, and they did. Cheating, treachery, murder and massacre, already a part of frontier trading, reached new heights, but still the hunt went on.

Sea otter herds were in serious decline on the north coast. This decline affected all traders, not just the Russians. The traders pressed the native hunters harder and harder to get pelts, requiring the hunters to travel over great distances. Accounts of native hunters being forced to paddle their *baidarkas* for hundreds of kilometres in filthy

This carved bowl by Henry
Hunt depicts a sea otter with a
sea urchin on its stomach.
COURTESY OF THE ROYAL
BRITISH COLUMBIA
MUSEUM, VICTORIA,
BRITISH COLUMBIA (CAT.
NO. 16613). REPRODUCED
BY PERMISSION OF
TONY HUNT.

weather without food or rest are part of the ugly story. Many died from exhaustion and exposure. Still the hunt went on. Even as late as 1802, seventeen thousand sea otter pelts were shipped from Alaska to Kamchatka. It was increasingly difficult to find new, unhunted herds.

An American trader from Boston knew that there were sea otters in California, but the same problem plagued him as it had others who sought to get their hands on the soft gold. He needed labour. The trader, a man named Joseph O'Cain, sailed north to approach a Russian by the name of Alexander Baranof and propose a partnership. O'Cain would supply the ship and Baranof would supply the hunters and *baidarkas*. O'Cain would take the hunters and their canoes on board his ship, sail to California, get the pelts and take them to the Orient. On his return, he would deliver the hunters and half the profits to Baranof in Alaska. The commercial sea otter hunt had come to California.

A look back through more than 250 years presents some remarkable parallels in the Bering and the Cook expeditions. Both voyages were undertaken to discover what lay beyond in an uncharted sea. Both were under the command of thoughtful, competent individuals of great skill. The expeditions were sponsored by the sovereign of each captain's country, and the captain of each died before his voyage was complete. Finally, the newly charted routes of both expeditions became maps to a gold mine, the rugged home of the sea otter.

THE END OF THE HUNT

The great sea otter hunt did not end on one day or even in one year. It died slowly and painfully, as the sea otter reached commercial extinction. Commercial extinction does not necessarily mean that the animal is biologically extinct; it simply means that in the world of commerce that animal no longer matters. It means that there are so few of the animals that the cost of hunting them cannot be justified by the meagre returns. This is what happens when animals are overhunted. One hopes that commercial extinction occurs before biological extinction, which is what happens when so many animals are killed that there are not enough to reproduce and carry on.

Commercial decline followed in the path of the fur hunters like a scavenger that stalks the stench of death. It moved from east to west along the Aleutian Islands, then trailed the fetid smell of slaughter on the American coast from north to south. By 1808, hunters had already abandoned the Aleutians. An experienced trader stopped in Cook Inlet in 1812 and only managed to get one hundred pelts, whereas before he had left with three thousand. It was worse in Prince William Sound, where hard hunting now produced a mere fifty skins; in the early days, there were fifty times that. Even hunters were becoming a thing of the past. A generation had passed, and many of the native hunters were gone—they had been killed or they had simply died. Their skills died with them when the next generation saw no benefit in working as slave labour for the Russians.

By the 1830s, the commercial sea otter hunt was finished in the North. Russian colonists hung on in Alaska by turning to shipbuilding and hunting fur seals. Eventually there seemed to be no good reason to support a losing proposition, and in 1867 Russia sold Alaska to the United States.

Alaska's new owners were quick to get back into the fur business. They started with the fur seals and moved on to sea otters, which had not been hunted during the last two or three decades of the Russian occupation of Alaska and thus had started to increase in numbers. After the hunting resumed, it wasn't long before the otters were virtually wiped out by a combination of highly mobile hunting parties and the best available rifles. The peace-loving little sea otter had been shot, speared, clubbed, trapped and netted from Bering Island to northern Mexico. It was gone, and the great sea otter hunt was over.

How big had the hunt actually been? How many animals had been slaughtered? How much money had been made? Nobody knows. There are a few clues to some numbers, and the rest is up to the imagination. From 1745 to 1822, for the Siberian/Aleutian run alone, 123 vessels are listed, with a declared total of 198,284 sea otter skins. These figures are from official records tabulated for collecting royal tribute. One can only wonder how accurate these numbers are, since the amounts were declared for the purpose of paying tax. What of the furs lost in dozens of shipwrecks, or pelts shipped directly to the Chinese market in later years, pelts traded to American and English ships, and all those that were smuggled? Those numbers will only add up to the Russian take of sea otters. How do we calculate the rest? How do we calculate the numbers for all the furs taken by American and English trading ships? What would the numbers mean if we knew what they were? What do half a million or two million sea otter pelts look like? Would they fill a boxcar, a house or something larger? What do a million skinned and bloody carcasses floating in the tidal foam look like? We can only imagine.

Hunters knew that sea otters
rafted together to rest in protected
bays and inlets.

NEXT PAGE: *Since sea otters
have no season of moult, as most
other fur bearers do, their coats
are always prime. As a result,
in the past sea otters were hunted
year round.*

CHAPTER 5

Sea Otters on the Move

By the early 1900s, nobody had seen a live sea otter for so long that many people thought they were extinct. But away from prying eyes, a few had survived in places so isolated and hidden that even the expert hunters of the past hadn't found them during the years of the great hunt. Quiet miracles occurred deep in hidden bays behind impassable reefs, as tiny sea otter pups were born to a very few otter mothers scattered in isolated pockets over thousands of kilometres of rocky shore. A year or two later, the miracle of birth was repeated. Thus, ever so slowly, small rafts of sea otters appeared where there had been none. The tenacious sea otter refused to surrender its right to exist.

When the sea otter received legislative protection in 1911, it became illegal to kill a sea otter or sell its pelt. Laws, however, are only as good as a society's ability to enforce them, and legal protection did not stop the killing. In his book *Hunters of the Stormy Sea*, the naturalist and explorer Harold McCracken writes:

> In 1916–17 when I spent my first winter among the Belkofski natives, repeatedly travelling in a small fur-trading schooner throughout the western coast region of the Alaska Peninsula, the sea otter was pretty generally supposed to be exterminated through Alaska, or so close to extinction that survival of the species was highly improbable. I found this to be untrue. Not only did I see otters in their native habitat of the kelp infested reefs, but I had an opportunity to buy pelts that had been poached for confidential sale, particularly to a San Francisco fur buyer who each spring made a trip on the monthly mail boat that travelled between Seward and Attu.

Even after the sea otter was given legal protection, there was a continuing interest in someday reinstating a fur industry based on the sea otter. Those were the days when

Ocean travel is part of a sea otter's life and may include journeys of a few kilometres to and from a good foraging site or a major seasonal migration of 50 kilometres (30 miles) or more.

every living thing, plant or animal, was judged according to its usefulness to people. Animals were categorized as "good" or "bad," good animals being ones that were useful as meat, hides or food for domestic animals. "Good" animals included deer, elk, lynx, ducks and food fish. "Bad" animals were ones that interfered in any way with human safety, comfort or agricultural productivity, such as wolves, coyotes and sea lions. Fish and game departments were charged with managing and protecting "good" wildlife species to maximize their use. They were equally responsible for eradicating "pest" species in control programs.

It is important to consider the scientific surveys of sea otters in the 1930s against this background. Investigations of Prince William Sound and the Aleutian Islands in the late 1930s confirmed that a few sea otters had survived the hunt and were reproducing. Amchitka Island appeared to have a thriving little population and was set aside as a sea otter sanctuary so that an accurate census of the animals could be taken and something could be learned about their habits and behaviour. This was truly a landmark event. Not since Steller sat with his note pad on his knee on windswept Bering Island in 1742 had anyone taken the time to observe, study and think about the sea otter as a marvellously adapted animal.

In the late 1940s, scientists observed that many sea otters were dying on Amchitka Island. Closer investigation of the dead animals revealed that it was not disease that was killing the animals, as had originally been thought, but starvation. Healthy adult animals were not among the dead; rather, the mortalities were old animals with severely worn teeth or young animals recently independent of their mothers. How could some animals starve in the same environment where others thrived? Eventually scientists concluded that the sea otter population on Amchitka Island had reached its maximum numbers for the food available. Large numbers of foraging otters had reduced the numbers of the most accessible and desirable food items, such as abalone, large sea urchins and crabs. With these items in short supply, otters were forced to eat more fish. Studies revealed that over half the diet of healthy otters was fish. To catch fish, a faster and more elusive prey, required speed, agility and strategy. Young animals probably lacked the skill to catch fish, and old animals probably lacked speed and stamina. Thus handicapped, these two groups would have had to make do with less nutritious food, such as immature sea urchins. Poorly nourished animals had even less energy to compete for what limited food there was, and so the young and the old were drawn into a vicious downward spiral, propelling them to eventual death from starvation.

Realizing that much of the sea otter's former range was empty of otters, biologists proposed moving some of the Amchitka otters to other areas where conditions were suitable and food was abundant. In 1951, thirty-five animals were captured and moved. All thirty-five animals died. In 1954, biologists tried again, and again the animals died. In 1955, more animals were captured and moved. All died. In 1956, however, of all the animals captured for translocation, only half died.

At this time, virtually nothing was known of the sea otter's biology or physiology. The relationship between the otter, its fur and the water, was not understood. Scientists did not know about the animal's high metabolic rate, daily food requirements, rapid digestion and inability to fast, as many terrestrial animals can.

Initial capture methods using nets were clumsy and wasteful. If the weather was bad, nets set to capture otters could not be tended and entangled otters died in desperate attempts to free themselves. Even though they could float at the surface entangled in the net, they could neither groom nor feed.

If an otter was retrieved alive from the nets, once out of water it was doomed. Soiled by its own excrement, the sea otter could not groom out of water. A coat that is soiled loses its waterproofing and soaks up water like a sponge. Wetted through, the coat becomes a dead weight and cold water soaks the animal's skin, draws off body heat and kills the animal with a lethal chill.

In some transport attempts, it was the reverse of chilling that killed the otters. Held out of water in poorly ventilated quarters, the otters became dangerously overheated. Trapped in their enormously thick coats, they had no way to cool off and so died of heat prostration.

Animals were not fed during transit, and consequently extended travel time meant long periods without food. For an animal that eats 25 per cent of its body weight every day, missing meals can be fatal. Enteritis, a gastric inflammation, quickly set in, killing more animals. Sea otters may be susceptible to enteritis because of their rapid digestion, which takes place in about two hours and which is probably also related to their large food intake and high metabolic rate.

In an attempt to avoid soiling, chilling, overheating and starvation, one transport operation tried moving the sea otters in water. A number of small pools were installed on the deck of the ship, and the otters were placed in these for the journey south. Initially all went well. To everyone's relief, the animals floated contentedly in their pools and ate well. Unfortunately, a storm at sea caused a terrible sloshing and washing in the small pools, and the otters could not orient themselves in the pools as the ship pitched and tossed. Had the animals been in the ocean, they would have ridden the swells. In their small pools, they were constantly thrown about. As a result, they became exhausted and could not groom themselves.

Many animals that survived capture, transport and release in a new location died soon after. The cumulative effects of so much stress simply could not be overcome.

As the translocation efforts of the 1950s failed again and again, the money and the will to continue to work died with many of the otters. Translocation might never have been attempted again were it not for a whole new set of circumstances that emerged in the 1960s.

The passionately held values of two generations collided when the United States government proposed to blow up nuclear weapons in the ocean, as a test, near Amchitka Island. The sixties generation was protesting weapons testing already, and when it was learned that wild sea otters, survivors of the terrible slaughter, lived at Amchitka Island, suddenly this far-off island that nobody had ever heard of became a very important place indeed. Sea otters had become almost a symbol to the fledgling environmental movement.

At the time, the sea otter was something of a media star in California, where for a long time it was thought to be extinct. In the mid-1930s, it became public that there was indeed a small group of wild sea otters near Big Sur, and slowly, over the years, the animals had multiplied. Now they could actually be watched and enjoyed by thousands of people standing on shore. As far as many people knew, California was the only place where a living wild sea otter could be seen.

The sea otter was a good news story, and the public embraced it. It was a story of survival against terrible odds, a testimony to stewardship over wanton destruction, a confirmation that good can triumph over evil. Here was a living example of a beautiful species that was thought to have been destroyed, gone from the Earth forever. To the conservation movement, the live sea otter represented a second chance at caring for an abused Earth. Imagine how well the conservationists received the news that an underground nuclear blast was planned for a place deep in the heart of wild sea otter territory.

In 1965, the United States exploded an underground nuclear blast near Amchitka Island. Although it was reported that the test did not disturb the otters, news of a much larger underground nuclear weapons test scheduled for 1968 drew strong criticism from environmental groups. Subsequently, the United States Atomic Energy Commission agreed to finance the translocation of large numbers of the island's sea otters before the blast. These translocations formed the second stage of sea otter transplants. Ironically, an invention designed to destroy life, the nuclear weapon, was the catalyst in a plan to ensure the sea otter's continued existence.

Fortunately, the 1968 blast did not take place until 1971, giving more time to

Sea otters travelled on board the
Canadian research vessel the
G.B. Reed *in one of the*
translocation projects. ANDY
LAMB

To avoid fouling their fur during transit, sea otters were placed in water-filled pools on board the ship. ANDY LAMB

remove otters. From 1965 to 1972, a number of federal and state agencies in the United States and provincial and federal agencies in Canada worked to move a total of 708 sea otters. In more than a dozen transplant operations, animals were collected from Amchitka and Prince William Sound, Alaska. Between 1965 and 1969, the majority, 412, were moved to other areas in Alaska: St. George Island in the Pribilof Islands and a number of islands and some mainland locations in southeastern Alaska. Three translocations, in 1969, 1970 and 1972, placed 89 sea otters in the Bunsby Islands off the west coast of Vancouver Island, British Columbia. Translocations in 1969 and 1970 placed 59 sea otters on the coast of Washington State. Finally, three groups of sea otters were relocated to two areas in the state of Oregon in 1970 and 1971.

The number of animals moved is not necessarily the number of animals that survived. In some cases, animals were known to be in poor shape when released; in others, where the sea otters were held in temporary pens and known to be eating and grooming before they were released, survival was probably high.

Through trial and error over more than two decades, the critical factors in the maintenance and transportation of sea otters were identified and methods were developed to capture, transport and release sea otters in good condition. Designing a transport crate, for example, was like solving a riddle. The sea otters required plenty of ventilation, but they also needed to be confined for their own safety during transport. The animals needed to eat but couldn't become fouled in excrement. They needed to be kept cool, but they couldn't risk chilling. Although sea otters are typically calm and nonaggressive, even when captured, they are physically strong and can chew through materials such as plastic with their strong jaws and teeth. Thus, a crate had to be escape-proof.

Many designs were developed, tried and improved upon. Finally, a crate was designed that fulfilled all requirements. Today sea otters can be transported anywhere in the world without risk or trauma to the animal. Many have been shipped from North America to as far away as Japan without incident.

Looking back on the huge mortalities suffered by these innocent animals at the hands of humans during the transplant operations, one cannot help but be deeply saddened and frustrated. Human ignorance was the real cause of these deaths. No one ever intended to kill so many animals, but that is what happened. It is further testimony to the tenacity of the sea otter that there were any survivors at all.

Were the transplant operations of the 1960s and 1970s successful? Although transplant attempts in the Pribilof Islands (1959, 1968) were thought to have failed, seven sea otters were seen there in 1988 and local residents claim there are many more in the

Biologists study the sea otter's behaviour by using spotting scopes and by tracking signals from tiny radio transmitters implanted in some animals.

area. It is not known if they have moved in from outside areas, such as Bristol Bay.

In southeastern Alaska, from an original 412 animals released between 1965 and 1969, a 1988 survey of the area sighted 4,500 animals between Dixon Entrance (parallel to Ketchican) in the south and Cape Spencer to the north (parallel to Glacier Bay). Biologists believe that the total number of sea otters actually in the area is nearer to 5,000 and that five times this number could live there as the sea otters expand into unoccupied areas.

In British Columbia, there has been similar success, though it has been slow in coming. Of the original 89 animals introduced, many were known to be in poor condition on release. About a decade after they were introduced, in 1978, it was estimated that there were only 70 to 120 animals. A survey in 1987 found 345 animals, and by 1992 the estimate stood at 600 sea otters, with new groups being found on the mainland and the Queen Charlotte Islands. Again, whether all these animals are the result of the transplants is not known. The coastline is long and thinly populated, and it is possible that a few animals from the original populations had survived unnoticed.

In Washington, two hundred sea otters were counted in a 1989 survey. Reviewing survey data from previous counts, and taking into account the number of dependent pups seen as a proportion of the whole group, biologists estimate the growth rate of this population to be about 20 per cent annually. This is similar to the estimated increases in British Columbia and Alaska (17 per cent and 18 per cent a year, respectively).

Unfortunately, in Oregon there is only bad news. Of the ninety-three animals released in 1970 and 1971, only twenty-one to twenty-three animals were sighted between 1972 and 1974. By 1981, only one animal was seen, and none have been seen since.

What happened to these animals? Some, perhaps all, may have died from a variety of causes. Some may simply have moved. Whereas humans may consider an area to be eminently suitable sea otter habitat, the sea otter may have quite different ideas. Biologists may look for areas that have an abundance of "sea otter food" and assume that sea otters will be content to live there. But the sea otter takes into account a complex suite of factors, food being an important factor but not the only one. In the end, we simply don't know why the sea otter has disappeared from Oregon.

There is yet another chapter, a third phase, in the sea otter transplant story, and it takes place in California. No sea otters have been introduced into California. Remember that California had its own relict population in the Big Sur area. By the mid 1930s, there were between fifty and three hundred sea otters in the region. This group continued to grow and, quite naturally, to expand north and south.

The "California" sea otter has been loved and despised. It has been accused of destroying the abalone fishery, pismo clam fishery and sea urchin fishery. It has been used to block offshore oil development and any number of other developments. Its high profile makes it a perfect pawn in political struggles, and its voracious appetite makes it a target for others exploiting marine food resources.

In contrast to the other translocation projects, which aimed to increase the sea otters' range, in California sea otters were moved to reduce their range. In 1969, seventeen animals from Cambria were captured and tagged and moved 72 kilometres (45 miles) north, back into sea otter territory. Nobody told the translocated otters that they were making a permanent move, however, and most were back in the Cambria area within the year.

In 1989, another nineteen sea otters were subjected to a similar move. This time they were transported 290 kilometres (180 miles), from Shell Beach in the southern part of their range north to Moss Landing, just north of Monterey. The rationale for the move was related to proposed oil development in the Santa Maria area. If a spill occurred, it was important to know how relocated otters would behave. Would they stay "relocated," or would they return, in this case to an oil-contaminated area?

As in the previous move, a number of sea otters returned to their original area, one covering the distance in only seven days. Half of the moved otters were held in floating pens for two days before they were released, and this delay affected their homing behaviour. Other factors, such as age, sex, presence of territorial males and time of year, seemed to influence the otters' movements as well.

Biologists studying the homing behaviour of sea otters have come to the conclusion that adults have an affinity for their home territory and that subadults, particularly males, are the most flexible and likely to disperse to new areas, looking for new opportunities. Studies of radio-tagged sea otters in Alaska reveal that newly independent sea otters may travel in excess of 100 kilometres (62 miles) from where they were last seen with their mothers. In fact, information on the movements of males and females, both

Photographer Jeff Foott with an
orphaned sea otter pup.

juveniles and adults, show that many otters travel seasonally and for much greater distances than was previously believed. Why they do this is not fully understood. Seasonal weather conditions are likely a factor in the north; a search for optimal conditions for rearing pups, seasonal abundance of food and avoiding predators could be factors as well.

In the early transplant operations, most animals were not tagged and so they could not be identified later. A follow-up study surveyed the transplant sites at irregular intervals, sometimes many years later, to count the animals present. As a result, the fate of most animals from the early moves is not known. One transplant operation, however, monitored the animals it moved. In this operation, the United States Fish and Wildlife Service undertook to reintroduce sea otters into San Nicolas Island in southern California. The operation began in 1987, and as of 1990, 136 individuals had been moved. All were marked with colour-coded flipper tags, and some were instrumented with radio transmitters. By June 1990, here is how they had fared: 15 stayed on the island; 30 returned to the mainland; 9 died from human-related causes, including capture stress; 3 were recaptured near the mainland and returned to their original home area; and 80 were unaccounted for.

If there is a central theme to the sea otter transplant story, it is this: it is not as easy as it looks, for the people or the sea otters. Some millions of years of evolution have equipped the sea otter to live in the ocean, but not just any piece of the ocean. Looking at the water's surface from land, one piece of ocean looks pretty much like every other piece of ocean. But to assume that the sea otter will simply live productively anywhere that it is set down on the coastal ocean would be the same as assuming that just because bears are terrestrial animals they will live anywhere on land. The coastal ocean is a complicated place, and the sea otter is a complicated animal. Perhaps if we take a more thoughtful and humble approach, the sea otter will teach us more about its world.

CHAPTER 6

A New Challenge

Sitting comfortably in our armchairs of the present, we study, analyze and finally pass judgement on events of the past. As we look back on our history with the sea otter, we are saddened at the loss of life and disgusted by the short-sighted greed that led to the near-extinction of the species. In the world of living things, however, dead is dead. An animal is no less dead if it died for a noble cause than if it was killed for greed. From a biological perspective, humans have simply been overefficient predators.

Before we judge the acts of those who went before us, we ought to squirm a bit in our cosy chairs because even today it is people who kill sea otters, both directly and indirectly. Otters that compete with commercial fish harvesters for the same species, such as abalone, are shot and clubbed to death. Fishers who set gill nets and trammel nets in sea otter areas drown many sea otters (as well as countless marine birds and other marine mammals, such as harbour porpoise and sea lions). In California, restrictions on net size and mesh openings and the closing of some fishing areas have helped to reduce, but not eliminate, the number of animals killed in nets.

At least the loss of sea otters—and other animals—in nets can be seen, studied and perhaps remedied. Less straightforward is the gradual accumulation in the oceans of pollutants and contaminants from land-based activities. Pesticides pour into the coastal ocean in runoff from agricultural lands. These come from many kilometres inland as they first seep into rivers and then flow to the sea. Organochlorides and some heavy metals progress through the marine food chain, becoming more concentrated with each transfer. Fuel and waste from marine traffic, industrial activities and municipal sewage outfalls all contribute to the degradation of the oceans.

Coastal communities and cities have traditionally used the oceans as a waste pit—out of sight, out of mind. Since the oceans have a remarkable capacity to renew themselves, the effects of contaminants went unnoticed for a long time. Even now the effects are dif-

With each passing year, sea otters are slowly returning to the kelp-rich coves where they once were so abundant.

ficult to study and costly to remedy. Ironically, the greatest effort to study a marine pollutant in the shortest period of time came as a result of an environmental nightmare.

THE <u>EXXON VALDEZ</u> OIL SPILL

On 24 March 1989, the American oil tanker the *Exxon Valdez* ran aground on Bligh Reef in Prince William Sound, Alaska, spilling over 41 million litres (11 million gallons) of crude oil into the sea. The slick eventually spread 700 kilometres (435 miles) to the southwest, affecting coastal areas along the Kanai Peninsula, Kodiak Archipelago and Alaska Peninsula. Wind and tide patterns determined which beaches would be soaked in oil and which would remain untouched. Not only were marine species affected but carrion feeders, such as bears, foxes, river otters and eagles, were contaminated when they came down to the shore to feed. Eagles, with their heads soaked in oil, returned to their nests and smeared oil on their nestling chicks as they groomed and tended them. At least 150 bald eagles died, and many nests did not fledge young that year.

It is estimated that over 100,000 marine birds perished when oil glued the hairs of their feathers together, destroying their waterproof jackets of thousands of exquisitely thin overlapping feathers covering the downy feathers below. The sea bird's outer feathers are remarkably similar to the sea otter's guard hairs in keeping the animal warm and dry. The oil also destroyed the waterproofing of the sea otter's fur, and cold water penetrated to the animal's skin. Although the animals responded by increasing their metabolic rate, hypothermia quickly set in. In a natural attempt to groom, the otters licked their fur and swallowed oil, causing severe kidney and liver damage. Breathing in the volatile elements of freshly spilled oil weakened their lung tissue, causing emphysema. Just over 1,000 oil-soaked carcasses were collected, comprising perhaps 30 to 50 per cent of the total killed.

Fish and wildlife agencies, conservation groups and the public worked together in rescue centres set up to help save the sea otters. A total of 361 animals were brought into the centres. Although many were in poor condition, just under half were only lightly oiled or not oiled at all. Eventually a total of 197 animals were released. A quarter of these were instrumented for follow-up studies. Over 18 million dollars was spent on sea otter rescue alone.

What percentage of a sea otter's fur must be affected before contamination becomes lethal? Some researchers say 10 per cent; some say 30 per cent. Everyone agrees, however, that sea otters are extremely vulnerable to oil contamination or contamination of any sort that affects the animal's fur. Yes, oiled otters can be washed. This means catching them, restraining them, anesthetizing them and then washing and rinsing them for two hours. The washing removes the sea otter's natural oils as well as the contaminating oil. The oil is gone, but the sea otters are still not waterproof. Two more weeks of nursing, feeding and constant care are required before release can be considered. All this added handling exerts additional stress. Some animals do survive, but are they affected over the long term? Nobody knows yet.

One could view the extraordinary cost of saving a few otters after the *Exxon Valdez* oil spill as an incredible waste of time, money, equipment, drugs and human resources. Was it worth it? For those who wanted to know beyond a shadow of a doubt that oil and otters don't mix, the answer is yes.

NEXT PAGE: A sea otter's fur is its "survival suit." Any floating oil or other pollutant that fouls the animal's fur means almost certain death for the otter.

THE THREAT OF THE DIVE FISHERIES

Except for abalone and pismo clams in California, sea otters have not competed with human harvesters until recently. The greater threat has traditionally been the fishing gear, not the species fished. This is because most fishers are interested in catching fish, and sea otters are not great fish eaters where there are lots of invertebrates to eat. This situation is starting to change, however. More and more, harvesters are turning to dive fisheries, exploiting species that were not previously hunted. (A dive fishery is one in which the animal cannot be harvested using nets, traps or lines and so divers are sent down to do the "fishing.") Each month a new species is added to the list, and in every case the animal is part of the sea otter's diet. To abalone and many kinds of clams, we can now add scallops, mussels, all species of crabs, sea urchins, sea cucumbers, octopus, and gooseneck barnacles.

It is difficult to find a single dive fishery that harvests selectively and responsibly. The usual situation is akin to strip mining, where every bit of the resource is taken. It does not take long for a species to become commercially extinct. When someone finally notices what has happened, there is the predicted outcry, with demands for regulation. Protection, enhancement and recovery of the damaged species then becomes the management and financial responsibility of a beleaguered fisheries department at the expense of the public purse. By then the divers have moved on to another area or another species, and the cycle repeats itself.

The situation poses a real threat to sea otters in two ways. The most obvious threat is the reduction of available food when any of the otter's prey species are being harvested by humans. This threat is very real. Sea otters will not be the first marine mammals to starve to death in their own environment. Consider the millions upon millions of tonnes of seafood products taken from the ocean in the Pacific Northwest every year. This fish is not "surplus"; it is part of a dynamic natural system that provides food for a host of animals in that system. Fortunately for fishers, what is going on in the ocean is hidden from view. If people can't see it, it doesn't exist. A similar raping of the land would never be tolerated.

A second threat to the sea otter posed by new dive fisheries is the notion that if people are earning a livelihood at something, they have the right to protect that livelihood under any circumstance. According to this way of thinking, sea otters are competitors and thus calls for their "control" are justified. That the sea otters were the first and that they have no other options, as human harvesters do, is never considered.

CELEBRATING A NEW ETHIC

Sea otters are defenceless against humans who wish to harm them, their environment or their food source. Their only protection is a caring public willing to take a stand on their behalf. It is important that people speak out on behalf of the sea otter, both for its own sake and for the sake of the thousands of other small animals that share its environment.

Someday, take your binoculars to a rocky coastal shore and watch the wild sea otters. Perch yourself on a sun-warmed rock and select an individual from the group. Watch what it is doing until you can push back the sounds of traffic and aircraft and imagine that you are there with the otters, the gulls, the sea lions and the killer whales as they were over two centuries ago.

As you look through your field glasses, you might spot an oversized brown powder puff, with a tiny black nose and two very blue eyes, cradled on its mother's chest in the bright morning sun. In this tiny animal, you can celebrate a victory over human greed and incredible odds. You can also celebrate a new ethic that acknowledges an animal's rights to food, space and peace. Today this baby otter sleeps today in its mother's arms, but its future is in our hands.

FOR FURTHER READING

NATURAL HISTORY AND BIOLOGY

Kenyon, Karl W. 1969. *The Sea Otter in the Eastern Pacific Ocean.* U.S. Fish and Wildlife Service, North American Fauna no. 68. Washington, D.C.

A classic on the subject of sea otters, this monograph is technical but readable.

Riedman, Marianne L., and James A. Estes. 1990. *The Sea Otter* (Enhydra lutris): *Behavior, Ecology and Natural History.* U.S. Fish and Wildlife Service Biological Report 90 (14). Washington, D.C.

A complete, up-to-date and highly readable though technical monograph on the sea otter.

Scheffer, Victor B. 1981. *The Amazing Sea Otter.* New York: Scribner's.

Although a great deal has been learned about the sea otter since this book was published, it remains a beautifully written story by a great naturalist/biologist.

Ford, Cory. 1966. *Where the Sea Breaks Its Back.* Boston: Little, Brown. Reprint. Anchorage and Seattle: Northwest Books, 1992.

An exciting and captivating version of Georg Steller's travels across Siberia and his experience on Bering's ill-fated voyage of discovery.

Golder, F. A. 1922–25. *Bering's Voyages.* American Geographical Society Research Series 1–2, New York.

Fascinating reading for those who wish to start at the beginning.

McCracken, Harold. 1957. *Hunters of the Stormy Sea.* Garden City, N.Y.: Doubleday.

This book picks up where Cory Ford's ends, at the beginning of the great hunt. The entire tale is told, with all the gory details.